What Shall We Do in a Hungry World?

Robert Parham

New Hope
Birmingham, Alabama

Unless otherwise indicated, Scripture quotations are from the *Revised Standard Version*.

New Hope
Birmingham, Alabama

Library of Congress Cataloging-in-Publication Data

Parham, Robert.
What shall we do in a hungry world? / Robert Parham. p. cm.
Bibliography: p.
ISBN: 0-936625-46-5: $4.95
1. Food supply— Religious aspects—Baptists. 2. Baptists—Southern States—Charities. I. Title.
HD9000.5.P267 1988
363.8'575'0973—dc 19 88-12397 CIP

N884106 • 7M • 0688

ACKNOWLEDGEMENTS

Permission to reprint portions of "The Faces of the Hungry Elderly in the Shadow of Plenty" from *Search* (Spring 1987) by Robert Parham has been granted by The Sunday School Board of the Southern Baptist Convention.

Permission to reprint portions of "The Hunger Issue in Southern Baptist Life: A Moral Consensus" (October 1987) by Robert Parham has been granted by *Baptist History and Heritage* of the Historical Commission of the Southern Baptist Convention.

To My Parents
Bob Parham
and
Jo Ann Walton Parham
who gave me an opportunity to see the world
and
a vision of what it could be

Contents

1. World Hunger Day: Old Commitments and New Challenges 1
2. God's Word in a Hungry World 10
3. Africa in Crisis 23
4. Hunger on the Home Front 38
5. The Best-Kept Secret 49
6. What Shall We Do? 59
7. On the Front Line: Three Special Christian Organizations 70

Preface

What shall we do in a hungry world? My family faced this question years ago when we lived in the Baptist Mission house outside Jos, Nigeria. By American standards, we did not have much material comfort. We did not even have electricity, except for a couple of hours every evening when the portable electric generator ran. But by Nigerian standards and those of the Third World, we were enormously wealthy.

Not surprisingly, an impoverished man came to our home asking for help. He explained in the Hausa language that one of his children had died and that another was very sick. He asked for help. My parents agreed. At dawn the next day, the man returned to our home with his wife and their son. The infant looked severely malnourished, an observation confirmed by a local missionary physician. Neither the physician nor my parents knew if the child's life could be saved, but they were determined to try. My father purchased the bottles, liquid vitamins, and powdered milk to feed the child. My mother taught the child's mother how to prepare formula and fed the child until he began gaining weight.

As a family with several young children, we talked about what to name this child. Roy Rogers, Gene Autry, and Tom Sawyer were suggested. We even considered naming this sticklike infant Jesus. In the end, we named him Sweet Pea.

Years later I realized that the consideration to name the child Jesus was not a silly, childish idea, but at the heart of the Christian message. I discovered the words of Jesus: "Truly, I say to you, as you did it to one of the least of these my brethren, you did it to me" (Matt. 25:40). I learned that at the core of the Christian faith is the idea that we are to respond to all as if responding to

Jesus himself. Back then, however, I was just a child full of curiosity about another child.

The story of Sweet Pea is an openended one. All we know about him is that he left our home as a healthy child, for we never saw him again. Yet the question he introduced into our lives still exists. The question my family faced almost 30 years ago is one that the Southern Baptist family faces today: What shall we do in a hungry world?

My book represents an effort to suggest answers to the question within the framework of the Southern Baptist Convention. It is written by a seventh-generation Baptist for Baptists on the eve of the tenth anniversary of World Hunger Day on the denomination's calendar. It is written to inform, to equip, and to challenge Southern Baptists to deepen their involvement in the movement against hunger in the upcoming decade.

A number of people have made this book possible. At the top of the list is my wife, Betsy Nunn. She gave me the freedom to work late at night, on weekends, and during vacation. Her special care for our preschool children Elisa and Christopher made the task easier. David Wilkinson, vice-president for seminary relations at the Southern Baptist Theological Seminary, acted as critic and encourager. Mary Tyler and Edith Wilson, Christian Life Commission secretaries, proofread and printed out numerous drafts. Others nettled, nudged, and nourished me along the way.

1
World Hunger Day: Old commitments and new challenges

Baptist pioneers

Southern Baptist concern about hunger is an old one. It reaches back to the early days of the denomination. People like Lottie Moon, L. L. Polk, C. T. Bailey, Annie Armstrong, and Clarence Jordan represent just a few of the Southern Baptists who have heard God's call to care for the poor and blazed a trail of involvement for others to follow. Their actions remind contemporary Southern Baptists about what we can do. Their diverse strategies point out the multiple ways we too may act in a hungry world.

Few individuals did more to inspire generations of Christians than did Lottie Moon (1840-1912), a Southern Baptist foreign missionary. Moon became an early missionary involved in hunger relief when she fed famine victims in China back in 1878. A few small gifts from the Foreign Mission Board of the SBC such as a single earring, a few stamps, and a handful of dollar bills were all the resources she had to share at her door.

When famine conditions spread in 1911, she wrote to a friend: "How can we bear to sit down to our bountiful tables and know of such things and not bestir ourselves to help? I hope you know that missionaries not only give their money but give their lives to help the famine stricken. Hardly ever did I know of a famine that did not claim its victims among missionaries."[1]

Her words were prophetic. By 1912 Lottie Moon was using her annuity payment to the Foreign Mission Board for famine relief.

She even stopped eating so others might eat. On Christmas Eve she died, weighing only 50 pounds, a victim of hunger.

Leonidas Lafayette Polk (1837-92) was a Southern Baptist of a different stripe from Moon. As a deacon at First Baptist Church, Raleigh, a North Carolina Baptist State Convention president (1889-90), and a member of the committee which recommended the founding of the Baptist Sunday School Board (1891), he was immersed in the denomination's work. But his heartbeat was not for foreign missions, it was for reform of the American economic system.

Following the Civil War, the South smoldered in ruin. Reconstruction accomplished little for farmers. Capital was lacking, farm prices were too low and costs were too high, and interest rates were suffocating. Farmers were becoming increasingly impoverished.

Against this backdrop of economic bad times, L. L. Polk determined to obtain relief through government action. He pushed a bill through the North Carolina legislature, establishing a state department of agriculture. Polk soon became the department's first commissioner (1877). Ten years later, he was still working against rural poverty. He started the magazine *Progressive Farmer* to help farmers help themselves and played a leading role in the founding of the North Carolina State College of Agriculture and Mechanic Arts (1888).

On the national scene, Polk served as the president of the Farmers Alliance (1889-92), an organization seeking to improve farm life. It was especially opposed to the concentration of financial power in the East and the inability of Congress to help. Speaking to Kansas farmers, Polk once declared:

> And in that great and final Day, when all the crime and misery shall be revealed, someone will have to answer for this lack of food. There is something besides overproduction that has caused it. Congress could give us a bill in forty-eight hours that would relieve us, but Wall Street says nay. . . . I believe that both of the parties are afraid of Wall Street."[2]

The failure of the Republican and Democratic parties to alleviate the hard times on the farm pushed the Farmers Alliance into the formation of the People's Party. Had Polk not died suddenly in 1892, he probably would have been its presidential candidate, campaigning for a graduated income tax, reform of antitrust laws, government control of transportation, and direct election of US senators. All objectives aimed at improving the lot of Americans most at risk to hunger and poverty.

Another North Carolina Baptist also expressed concern about the poor, but his focus was on the local church. C. T. Bailey, editor of the *Biblical Recorder,* wrote in 1892: "The reputation of caring for the poor is one that the church ought to covet, and one that she cannot afford to dispense with, if she would fulfill her true mission on earth." He believed a sign of true Christianity was that "institutions for the relief of the poor and destitute abound." Bailey even urged North Carolina Baptist churches to establish a "poor fund."[3]

Bailey's belief found expression in the ministries of the Woman's Missionary Union (WMU) which from its earliest days engaged in charitable activities such as caring for the sick and underprivileged. One of WMU's founders, Annie Armstrong, for example, gave lectures on "family budgeting and meal planning for persons with low incomes."[4] Armstrong surely knew that helping the poor in such areas was one solution to the prevention of domestic hunger.

The most dramatic approach to meeting human needs appeared in an experiment called Koinonia Farm which began in 1942 with the purchase of a 440 acre run-down farmstead southwest of Americus, Georgia. At the heartbeat of the endeavor to create a Christian community resembling the New Testament community was Clarence Jordan (1912-68). His undergraduate degree in agriculture from the University of Georgia and a ThD degree in Greek New Testament from the Southern Baptist Theological Seminary made him uniquely qualified to help the rural poor and to translate the Bible into a plain English version known as the Cotton Patch Version.

In addition to racial reconciliation, Jordan and others sought radical stewardship, the kind of stewardship practiced by the early church. They believed that to follow Jesus meant giving up everything, holding income and property in common, and distributing resources to meet the needs of the poor. What they believed, they lived out in many ways, including sharing agricultural knowledge with poor farmers, as well as starting a Fund for Humanity designed to empower the poor.[5] (See the chapter entitled "On the Front Lines: Three Special Christian Organizations" for the discussion on Habitat for Humanity.)

Moon, Polk, Bailey, Armstrong, and Jordan represent the believers who have come before modern-day Southern Baptists. Their strategies for meeting hunger needs differ sharply, yet their commitments to respond are strikingly similar.

The beginning of a new Baptist commitment

While individuals and groups of Southern Baptists have had a deep concern about hunger, it was not until the early 1970s that the issue caught fire across the denomination. News stories in the early 1970s about the starvation in Sahel, the band of land through Africa just below the Sahara Desert, pinched a moral nerve among Southern Baptists. Reports about hunger in India and Bangladesh added pressure.

Southern Baptists saw television images of skeletal human beings with swollen bellies, reddish skin, and gaunt eyes. Their eyes met our eyes. Their outstretched hands touched our tender hearts. And we responded.

The first thing Southern Baptists did when we gathered for state conventions in 1974 was to resolve to fight hunger. Texas Baptists resolved "to miss one meal each week in 1975 and give instead at least one dollar for that meal to the Southern Baptist Foreign Mission Board for world hunger needs."[6] Similar resolutions were passed in state conventions meeting in Florida, Kentucky, and North Carolina. Florida Baptists also set aside March 18, 1975, as World Hunger Sunday to collect a hunger offering.

On the heels of state convention resolutions came a string of awareness-raising and action-oriented activities. In December 1974 the Christian Life Commission of the Baptist General Convention of Texas mailed a 16-page packet to pastors to help them address the issue. The executive-secretary of the North Carolina Convention in mid-January 1975 challenged Baptists in his state to raise $100,000 in 30 days for world hunger. They gave over $258,000 in 10 months. In October 1975 the Virginia Baptist Convention mailed out a hunger awareness packet, supporting national legislation concerning the right to food and recommending the purchase of a book entitled *Bread for the World.*

The editors of missions magazines *World Mission Journal, Home Missions, The Commission, Royal Service,* and *Contempo* devoted numerous pages from the spring of 1975 to the summer of 1976 to the hunger crisis and what Southern Baptists were doing and could do. In the fall of 1975 the National Student Ministries Department of the Baptist Sunday School Board mailed a hunger resource kit to student leaders and set a fund-raising goal for a hunger project in Bangladesh. The Christian Life Commission of the SBC began offering substantive leadership in January 1976 when it mailed out thousands of hunger awareness/action packets.

Adding significant leadership were several grass-roots organizations, one of which was the Agricultural Mission Foundation based in Yazoo City, Mississippi, and headed by Owen Cooper, a former SBC president. A grant from this organization enabled the Radio and Television Commission to produce a hunger film entitled *Struggle for Survival*.

Another group was the hunger committee of Oakhurst Baptist Church in Decatur, Georgia. It began a newsletter called *Seeds* for Southern Baptists concerned about hunger. The newsletter grew into a monthly magazine, and then into a nationally recognized hunger publication. (See the chapter entitled "On the Front Lines: Three Special Christian Organizations" for the discussion on *Seeds*.)

In the fall of 1978 the Foreign Mission Board, Home Mission Board, Sunday School Board, Woman's Missionary Union, Brotherhood Commission, Baptist Joint Committee on Public Affairs, Baptist World Alliance, and Christian Life Commission sponsored a hunger convocation at Ridgecrest, North Carolina. For two days, 250 Southern Baptists listened, debated, and then recommended a number of courses of action.

One recommendation was that the observance of World Hunger Day be moved from August to a more prominent date and that it be aggressively promoted. A year earlier the 1977 SBC had approved a recommendation from the Denominational Calendar Committee that World Hunger Day be observed on the first Wednesday in August, beginning in 1978. World Hunger Day continued to be observed on a Wednesday in August until the Denominational Calendar Committee recommended in 1979 that the date be changed to the second Sunday in October, beginning in 1981.

A new moral consensus

Southern Baptists now have a moral consensus that feeding hungry people is one of the issues at the core of the biblical message and at the heart of the Baptist mission. Evidence of this consensus is found in the rapid way in which the issue has advanced from the periphery to the mainstream of ethical concerns in a denomination known for its conservatism. Financial contributions, institutional commitments, and writing about hunger are just a few of the pieces of evidence.

Financial contributions to worldwide hunger through the Foreign and Home Mission Boards surged from $299,925 in 1974 to an all-time high of $11,830,146 in 1985, despite the fact that the SBC does not have a promotional program specifically for raising hunger funds. The spectacular leap in giving would be even more impressive if a mechanism existed to measure hunger gifts which are allocated for use in the local church, association, and state convention.

Institutional commitments at the SBC and state Baptist convention levels are substantial. The Foreign Mission Board in 1988 had 50 agricultural missionaries in 32 different countries and 156 hunger relief projects in 41 nations. The Home Mission Board distributed hunger funds in nearly every state and the District of Columbia.

Numerous examples of the growth of institutional commitments also exist at the state convention level. The Kentucky Baptist Convention is sponsoring four regional workshops each year for five years (1986-90) on how to meet human needs. In Louisiana the convention's World Hunger Committee publishes a quarterly newsletter on the issue. Another world hunger committee is active in the Arkansas Baptist Convention.

Writing about hunger has spiraled upward in the last decade. A review of the *Southern Baptist Periodical Index* indicates the number of articles under the entry of Hunger increased from a total of eight between 1970 and 1974 to 247 between 1980 and 1984. While data on Baptist Press stories dealing with hunger is incomplete, more stories are carried on hunger than on any other social issue.

The next decade of challenges for Baptists

Today Southern Baptists lock arms in agreement about the biblical message to feed the hungry and the necessity for mission boards to conduct hunger ministries. We stand arm in arm in agreement that we ought to observe World Hunger Day and give to the cause of hunger relief and development. We have made important gains. But worldwide hunger challenges Southern Baptists to deepen involvement in four areas in the next decade.

First, we must restudy the Bible. Baptists claim to be people of the Book. We believe the Bible is the authoritative written word from God. We affirm that the Bible is a flawless treasure of divine instruction. We acknowledge that the Bible is a wellspring of truth for Christian living.

Despite all our affirmations, too often too many Christians talk too much about the Bible, rather than spending time reading it. Restudying the Bible, with a special eye on the issue of hunger, may enable believers to see what God wants, to hear His call to care for the poor, the outcast, the weak.

Second, we must rethink the issue of hunger. We need to understand hunger as a chronic reality born of man-made problems, not just an acute crisis born of nature. The lack of rain can cause hunger. Poverty, deforestation, mismanagement, civil strife, economic failure, overgrazing of livestocks, and ill-designed foreign aid projects can also cause hunger.

Consider the fact that the drought in Sahel "began" in 1983. Yet in 1983 and 1984 the countries of Burkina Faso, Chad, Mali, Niger, and Senegal, all of which faced widespread hunger, produced a record harvest of cotton while also setting a record for imported cereal foods. Why can these nations grow an export crop but not grain in a drought season? Did hunger in these countries result more from the nature of African agriculture than the lack of rain?

Beside how we understand the causes of hunger, we need to reflect on what compels us to respond. For example, Americans are far more interested in scrambling to respond to disaster, such as drought, than to working methodically on deep political, economic, and environmental problems. We tend to view disasters as those events beyond human responsibility. Disasters are acts of nature. We feel good about helping victims of natural disasters, but we are far less confident about helping victims of man-made problems. Yet natural disasters are far less destructive than social disasters.

The chronic hunger of 730 million people results from man-made problems. People who face hunger on a daily basis need aid as much as drought victims do. In fact a recent study has estimated that "all major disasters throughout the 1970s killed over 142,000 people a year on the average. Yet each year some 15 million children die of malnutrition-related causes, and nowhere is this carnage described as a disaster."[7] We need to understand that hunger is a daily problem, not just a problem when nature goes mad.

Another dimension to the way we think about hunger is our reliance on news reports to spark a response. Records indicate that when hunger is in the news, contributions go up. When hunger stories move from the front page to the back page to off the page, contributions fall sharply. We need to remember that world hunger day is every day.

Third, we must reexamine our involvement in public policy. Southern Baptists stride aggressively into the public arena to oppose gambling and liquor-by-the-drink, yet we rarely speak with confidence for or against legislation concerning the hungry. If we are going to make a difference, then we must broaden our citizenship agenda to include hunger issues.

President Ronald Reagan said that a hungry child knows no politics. He was absolutely right. But politicians know that hungry children do not vote, do not lobby, do not have political action committees, and do not have political power. What hungry children ought to have are Christian advocates pleading their case before the bar of public policy.

Advocacy for the hungry is a form of Christian faithfulness and witnessing. It enables Christians to fulfill our responsibility to care for the weak. It informs secular government what moral values we hold and want society to practice.

One of the great ironies is that US congressmen and senators from the Bible Belt consistently have among the worst voting records on hunger and poverty issues. The Bible speaks clearly to the hunger issue, but those who claim to read the Bible most often are not speaking clearly to their elected officials. Southern Baptists must make Christian citizenship as commonplace as Christian charity (benevolence). We must use public policy to remove the barriers which keep people poor and to build bridges across the river from the land of destitution and dependence to the land of self-reliance.

Fourth, we must readjust our life-styles. If we are going to feed a hungry world, then we must look at how we live compared to how others live.

Life-style adjustment involves many areas. How much do we spend on ourselves? How often do we buy new clothes or cars? How much do we give to our local church? How much do we give to feed the hungry and to help them feed themselves?

To increase our impact in a hungry world, we must give more than 63 cents per person as Southern Baptists through the Foreign and Home Mission Boards. The amount we give to the hunger ministries of the Foreign and Home Mission Boards is less than the cost of two candy bars. Many people have felt that a goal of $1 per person is within our immediate reach.

Others have much larger visions. William Pinson, executive secretary of the Baptist General Convention of Texas, has said: "If only one out of 20 Southern Baptists gave just $10 per month to the hungry, our annual SBC offering would exceed $84 million. Never in our history as a convention have we even approached this amount."[8]

We must readjust our life-styles in order that others might have a chance to live. The Catholic saint Anne Seton said, "Live simply that others may simply live." It is a good motto. It may also be one of the most profound testimonies to Christ.

[1]Catherine B. Allen, *The New Lottie Moon Story* (Nashville: Broadman Press, 1980), 270.

[2]Lawrence Goodwyn, *Democratic Promise: The Populist Movement in America* (New York: Oxford University Press, 1976), 193-94.

[3]C. T. Bailey, "Caring for the Poor," *Biblical Recorder,* May 25, 1892.

[4]Catherine B. Allen, "Other Issues Needing Attention," *Baptist History and Heritage* 22 (July 1987): 39.

[5]Dallas Lee, *The Cotton Patch Evidence* (New York: Harper and Row, Publishers, 1971).

[6]*Annual*, Baptist General Convention of Texas, 1974, 25.

[7]Anders Wijkman and Lloyd Timberlake, *Natural Disasters: Acts of God or Acts of Man?* (Washington, D. C.: International Institute for Environmental and Development, 1984), 4.

[8]William Pinson, "Hunger Is Not Seasonal," *Baptist Standard,* October 9, 1985, 7.

2
God's Word in a hungry world

By the year 2000, 60 million abandoned street children will live in major city ghettos in Latin America. Two billion people will suffer from chronic malnutrition. The gap between the very rich and very poor will become a chasm. The world's wood stock will decline 47 percent, deserts will claim greater stretches of cropland, and water supplies will diminish drastically.[1]

The forecast is grim. The world is hungry, and it may become even hungrier. Were it not for God's message in sacred Scripture about care for the weak, the vulnerable, and the dispossessed, many Christians simply would retreat. But God's message calls Christians into, not to escape from, the challenges of the world.

Studying what the Bible says about hunger is a prerequisite for Christian action in the world, for the Bible is a treasure chest of divine instruction. The Bible points out that hunger has always been part of the drama of sinful humanity. It says that the covenant community has a responsibility for the weakest members of society, many of whom are either ignored or trampled on by the people of God. It shows that God's only Son fed the hungry, associated with the poor, and set up a new economic life-style. It discloses that even the new Israel was stalked by hunger.

Jack Nelson, author of *Hunger for Justice: The Politics of Food and Faith*, has written: "Despite a disparity of several thousand years, the description of the economic roots of hunger in the Bible is helpful in shaping our understanding of the present world food crisis."[2] Indeed the Bible remains as relevant about social problems today as it did yesterday.

Who were the hungry in biblical times?

The Bible offers two descriptions of hunger: one is famine, the other is chronic hunger which exists day in and day out.

Famine

Famine occurred over and over again in biblical times. Abraham, Jacob, Joseph, Moses, Ruth, numerous kings, and early Christians felt the scorching heat of severe hunger. The author of Lamentations captured the dreadful experience of starvation when he wrote: "Our skin is hot as an oven with the burning heat of famine" (Lam. 5:10).

Part of the early story of God's chosen people revolved around recurring famine. Abram escaped the harsh famine conditions with a sojourn to Egypt (Gen. 12:10). Much later his great-grandson Joseph interpreted the dream of Pharaoh which forewarned about seven years of famine and enabled the Egyptians to prepare for the coming food crisis (Gen. 41:25-36). Learning of the food reserves, Jacob told his sons: "Behold, I have heard that there is grain in Egypt; go down and buy grain for us there, that we may live, and not die" (Gen. 42:2). The obedience of his sons placed in motion events which would lead to Jacob's family settling in the land of Goshen.

Famine scorched the land in the days of the kings. Once a drought was so severe in Samaria that King Ahab told his servant Obadiah to "go through the land to all the springs of water and to all the valleys; perhaps we may find grass and save the horses and mules alive, and not lose some of the animals" (1 Kings 18:5).

On another occasion, war caused famine. When King Benhadad of Syria encircled Samaria, he cut off the food supply: "And there was a great famine in Samaria, as they besieged it, until an ass's head was sold for eighty shekels of silver, and the fourth part of a kab of dove's dung for five shekels of silver" (2 Kings 6:25). This desperate situation resulted in cannibalism, as evidenced by the starving woman who cried to the king of Israel: "We boiled my son, and ate him" (2 Kings 6:29).

The horrible siege and destruction of Jerusalem in 586 B.C. created a famine: "Happier were the victims of the sword than the victims of hunger, who pined away, stricken by want of the fruits of the field. The hands of compassionate women have boiled their own children; they became their food in the destruction of the daughter of my people" (Lam. 4:9-10).

Famine was just one description of hunger in biblical times. It arose from drought and war, and it affected everyone, the rich and the poor. Another description was that of chronic hunger arising from poverty. The biblical writers recognized that the poor were those most vulnerable to hunger.

Chronic hunger

The sojourner, the fatherless, and the widow were among the people most at risk to poverty and consequently to hunger. Their plight arose from the fact that they had no legal status. The sojourner was a foreigner living in Israel; the orphan and the widow had no protector or provider.

Seeing their vulnerability, Moses repeatedly told the people to care for them. His rationale was simple: As God had heard the cries of the slaves in Egypt and had come to their rescue, so too does God deliver others who suffer, and expects the covenant people to do likewise.

"He [God] executes justice for the fatherless and the widow, and loves the sojourner, giving him food and clothing," Moses said. "Love the sojourner therefore; for you were sojourners in the land of Egypt" (Deut. 10:18-19). Again, Moses urged: "You shall not pervert the justice due to the sojourner or to the fatherless, or take a widow's garment in pledge; but you shall remember that you were a slave in Egypt and the Lord your God redeemed you from there" (Deut. 24:17-18).

The consequence of ignoring the weak was severe. "Cursed be he," Moses said, "who perverts the justice due to the sojourner, the fatherless, and the widow" (Deut. 27:19). Elsewhere Moses warned: "You shall not wrong a stranger or oppress him, for you were strangers in the land of Egypt. You shall not afflict any widow or orphan. If you do afflict them, and they cry out to me, I will surely hear their cry; and my wrath will burn." (Ex. 22:21-23).

Moses left a deep imprint on Israel. Again and again, the biblical authors identified the same list of needy people and called repeatedly for their care. The biblical writers reminded the people that God looked after orphans and widows (Psalm 68:5-6) and did not want them mistreated (Jer. 22:1-5 and Zech. 7:8-14).

Like the Old Testament, the New Testament links poverty and hunger. One biblical scholar, Wolfgang Stegemann, believes that in the New Testament "poverty is synonymous with being hungry."[3] He contends: "The face of poverty . . . is basically this: the poor are destitute, always close to starvation, often identified along with the disabled and the severely ill, poorly clothed, and dependent on the help of strangers."[4]

Indeed, the poor frequently faced hunger. One sabbath as the disciples walked through the grain fields, their hunger compelled them to pluck, sift, and eat the grain. Apparently they were too impoverished to have prepared food for the sabbath as was the custom (Luke 6:1-6). On another occasion, the disciples and a crowd of followers faced a lack of food (Luke 9:10-17). On other occasions, Jesus saw that the poor, maimed, lame, blind (Luke 14:12-14), and beggars (Luke 16:19-31) were among the hungry.

Even members of the early church were poverty stricken. The widows in the Jerusalem church needed a daily distribution of food (Acts 6:1). In fact, the entire Jerusalem church was so poor that Paul collected an offering for them from among the Gentile Christian churches (Gal. 2:10; Rom. 15:22-33; 1 Cor. 16:1-4; and 2 Cor. 8-9).

Again and again, the community of faith is assigned the task of feeding the hungry and helping the hungry feed themselves.

What does the Old Testament say about feeding the hungry?

The Old Testament urges the covenant people to look after the hungry in concrete ways. One of the most straightforward set of instructions for the prevention of hunger is the law of gleaning; another is the observance of the sabbatical year; a third is the pursuit of justice.

The law of gleaning

The law of gleaning prevented the Hebrew farmer from taking all the produce out of his fields, vineyard, or orchard. When harvesttime came, the reapers worked their way through the field gathering the produce. Behind them followed the poor, picking up what was left behind. The leftovers belonged to the poor, for the law instructed the owner of the farm not to pick the field clean.

Moses instructed the people: "When you reap the harvest of your land, you shall not reap your field to its very border, neither shall you gather the gleanings after your harvest. And you shall not strip your vineyard bare, neither shall you gather the fallen grapes of your vineyard; you shall leave them for the poor and the sojourner: I am the Lord your God" (Lev. 19:9-10).

Another set of similar yet more explicit instructions were also offered in Deuteronomy 24:19-21.

The best known biblical account of gleaning involved Ruth (Ruth 2:2-23). When Naomi and Ruth went to Bethlehem at the beginning of harvesttime, they faced hunger. So Ruth volunteered to go into the fields to collect the stalks of grain left behind.

The law of gleaning was clearly in effect (Ruth 2:2). Yet Ruth asked the foreman at dawn: "Pray, let me glean and gather among the sheaves after the reapers" (Ruth 2:7). Why did she ask for permission to follow the law? Did her request indicate that some hard-hearted farmers refused to let the poor glean their fields? Did certain landlords try to squeeze every bit of profit out of their fields? Did some farmers break the law and thereby contribute to poverty and hunger?

If some landowners were breaking the law of gleaning, Boaz's foreman was not. He granted Ruth permission, and she gleaned from sunup to sunset. At the end of the day, she had an ephah, or a bushel, of barley. The law of gleaning had enabled the great-grandmother of King David to avoid hunger.

The sabbatical year

Another concrete program to prevent poverty was the sabbatical year (Deut. 15:1-18). It was an effort to protect the poor, ensuring the welfare of all within the covenant community.

At the end of a cycle of seven years came the "year of dropping" or "year of cancellation." Creditors were to release debts (Deut. 15:1-11) and slaveholders were to free slaves (Deut. 15:12-18). If God's law was obeyed, Moses said, "there will be no poor among you" (Deut. 15:4) and the entire nation would be blessed.

The first feature of the sabbatical year was the cancellation of debt. "Every creditor shall release what he has lent to his neighbor" (Deut. 15:2), Moses instructed. He warned creditors against pressing hard to collect debts. The justification for such an economic program was simple: God had proclaimed it.

Moses added that discrimination against the poor was unacceptable: "If there is among you a poor man . . . you shall not harden your heart or shut your hand against your poor brother, but you shall open your hand to him, and lend him sufficient for his need" (Deut. 15:7-8). Risk was not to be a reason to refuse making a loan. Neither was the approach of the sabbatical year a justification for refusing to lend to a needy man (Deut. 15:9).

The attitude of the lender was another concern: "Take heed lest there be a base thought in your heart" (Deut. 15:9), and "your heart shall not be grudging when you give to him" (Deut. 15:10). The people of the covenant were to care genuinely for the poor, not just obey the law.

The second feature of the sabbatical year was the release of slaves. In biblical times people fell into slavery for many reasons, one of which was economic failure. If an Israelite became a slave, he labored for six years and was set free on the seventh.

A slave was not just set free. He was freed and given the resources to look after himself: "And when you let him go free from you, you shall not let him go empty-handed." Instead the slaveholder was instructed, "you shall furnish him liberally out of your flock, out of your threshing floor, and out of your wine press" (Deut. 15:13-14).

The reason for such action was straightforward. The economic well-being of the former slave contributed to the economic well-being of the entire nation. When the nation prospered, the former slaveowner would experience God's blessing (Deut. 15:18).

When Moses set forth his antipoverty program, he said that if the sabbatical year was followed, then the nation would be void of poverty (Deut. 15:4). He envisioned a nation without hunger. Yet Moses knew the effects of human sinfulness and social evil. He recognized the entrenched, long-lasting nature of poverty (Deut. 15:11). The reality of poverty demanded a continuous effort to eliminate it.

Accompanying the law of the sabbath was the year of jubilee (Lev. 25:10-24). Every 50 years, liberty was proclaimed "throughout the land to all its inhabitants." Enslaved Israelites were released; property was returned to its original owner. Such leveling of the economic system assured that the poor would be able to look after themselves (Luke 4:19).

The sabbatical year, as well as the year of jubilee, existed so that "the poor . . . people may eat" (Exo. 23:10-11). As often was the case, however, the people of Israel ignored the law of Moses. Their failure to keep the law of the sabbatical year resulted in poverty. It eventually contributed to the captivity in Babylon (Jer. 34:8-22 and 2 Chron. 36:20-21).

Pursuit of justice

The Old Testament writers were painfully aware of social injustice. Many saw its harmful impact. Some even experienced its crushing hand. All knew that social injustice stood against the God of justice.

Indeed, God was portrayed as "a God of justice" (Isa. 30:18). "The Lord loves justice" (Isa. 61:8). (See also Psalms 33:5; 37:28). Other biblical authors wrote that God heard the cries of those treated unjustly (Psalm 109:21), executed justice for the needy (Psalm 140:13), and called the whole nation to pursue justice (Deut. 16:20). The first part of Micah's answer to his classical question about what the Lord required was straightforward: "Do justice" (Micah 6:8).

The Old Testament writers knew of both the nature of God and social injustice. Amos, for example, saw that social injustice caused hunger. He knew what was happening in the marketplace. He knew that the wealthy sold "the righteous for silver, and the needy for a pair of shoes" (Amos 2:6). He saw that the poor were trampled "into the dust of the earth" (Amos 2:7). He recognized that the greedy appetites of wealthy women caused great suffering (Amos 4:1).

As a herdsman and picker of sycamore fruit (a food of the poor), Amos had firsthand experience in the marketplace. He caught on that in the market the wealthy cheated poor farmers out of their wheat, then built expensive homes for themselves (Amos 5:11). He figured out that the scales were fixed, that the poor paid more for less food, and that the quality of food was marginal (Amos 8:6). Undoubtedly, Amos realized that lavish life-styles of a few ground down the poor.[5]

Other prophets also pointed out injustice. "Like the partridge that gathers a brood which she did not hatch," Jeremiah wrote, "so is he who gets riches but not by right" (Jer. 17:11).

The counterbalance to the destructive nature of social injustice was justice. Thus, Moses, for example, gave a legal code which urged the people not to steal, not to deal falsely, and not to oppress a neighbor, as well as to pay a worker his rightful wages and to be fair (Lev. 19:11-18). Knowing of the deceitful heart of humanity, Moses spoke against cheating in the marketplace: "You shall do no wrong in judgment, in measures of length or weight or quantity. You shall have just balances, just weights, a just ephah, and a just hin" (Lev. 19:35-36). His desire for fairness in the market echoed through the ages (Deut. 25:13-16; Prov. 11:1, 16:11; Amos 8:5).

Besides speaking against injustice, the biblical writers stressed the benefits of social justice. They pointed out that justice made for social stability (Prov. 29:4), governmental stability (Prov. 16:12; 29:14), and social prosperity (Psalm 72:2, 4, 16). The pursuit of justice was in the self-interest of the entire nation.

More importantly, social justice evidenced a right relationship with God. Moses, Amos, and Isaiah all believed that justice and right worship were different sides of the same coin. In Moses' farewell speech to the tribes of Israel, he reminded the people about rejoicing before the Lord (a form of worship) and following "justice, and only justice" (Deut. 16:10-20).

Amos made a similar link between worship and justice. Speaking for the Lord, Amos said: "I hate, I despise your feasts, and I take no delight in your solemn assemblies" (Amos 5:21). Rather than false worship, what the Lord wanted, Amos said, was that "justice roll down like waters, and righteousness like an ever-flowing stream" (Amos 5:24).

The prophet Isaiah also harnessed right worship and justice (Isa. 1:1-17). He shared a vision in which the Lord said: "I have had enough of burnt offerings of rams and the fat of fed beasts; I do not delight in the blood of bulls, or of lambs, or of he-goats" (Isa. 1:11). God no longer found the worship of the people acceptable (Isa. 1:14-17).

Isaiah's vision from God clearly tied right living with right worship. The vision condemned the pious who offered all the right signs of worship, except for a genuine care for the poor. Such religious people engaged in false worship (Isa. 58:1-9).

What does the New Testament say about feeding the hungry?

The New Testament evidences greater concern about poverty and hunger than is generally acknowledged. Certainly, Jesus addresses and meets human needs. And the early church follows His path through the practice of hunger aid within and between churches.

The life and words of Jesus

Poverty surrounded Jesus from the very start. He was born into a hungry world, but in a town whose very name means "house of bread." And Mary's miraculous conception of Him paled in the filthy conditions in which she delivered Jesus.

Adding to the picture of poverty was the event of consecration. When time came to dedicate Jesus to the service of God and for the cleansing of Mary, his parents were too poor to afford a respectable offering (Luke 2:21-24). They had to make a poor man's offering of "two turtledoves" (Lev. 12:6-8).

Poverty remained an integral feature of Jesus' life. Even Jesus' first temptation in the wilderness mocked His life in poverty. The Devil's temptation was for Jesus to look after His own needs first by turning stones to bread. But Jesus resisted. He knew the importance of bread for human life, as well as the importance of obedience to God, even if it involved physical hunger (Luke 4:1-4). In all likelihood, Jesus' early beginnings and hunger pangs in the wilderness deepened His desire to provide a banquet for the hungry (Deut 8:3).

Jesus' first recorded sermon in the synagogue of Nazareth disclosed His mission: "The Spirit of the Lord is upon me, because he has anointed me to preach good news to the poor. He has sent me to proclaim release to the captives and recovering of sight to the blind, to set at liberty those who are oppressed, to proclaim the acceptable year of the Lord" (Luke 4:18-19).

The congregation responded with amazement. They were unable to believe that this man had come to restart the year of jubilee. The Jewish community had long since stopped practicing the sabbatical year and the year of jubilee. Debts were no longer cancelled and slaves were no longer freed (Lev. 25).

At first, the people were struck by the vision of jubilee. But as the weight of His message hit home, their attitude changed. To return the economic system to the Mosaic ideals was too threatening. The people did not want the existing economic order overturned, even if it meant helping the downtrodden. Not surprisingly, their response was unfavorable (Luke 4:20-30).

As Jesus moved through the country, He continued to address hunger needs (Luke 6:1-5, 20-21; 11:3; and 14:12-14). Nowhere was this relationship more vividly illustrated than in the feeding of the 5,000. By the time of this event, Jesus was attracting a large following. Many of them were poor and handicapped (Matt. 15:30). Their inability to feed themselves troubled the disciples to the point of trying to persuade Jesus to send them away to look after themselves. Jesus refused.

"You give them something to eat," He said to the disciples (Luke 9:13). They responded with complaints of limited resources. Yet Jesus rejected their excuses with the message that He wanted the hungry to receive food (Luke 9:10-17).

Accompanying Jesus' message about love of neighbor was a word about judgment. Jesus painted a picture of a man named Lazarus who died outside the residence of a wealthy man. Apparently, the wealthy man did nothing to help the beggar beyond throwing him a few scraps. The rich man was judged for neglecting Lazarus's needs (Luke 16:19-31).

Another aspect of Jesus' message concerned conversion. True conversion resulted in care for others, including economic care. When a rich ruler, who had kept the commandments, wanted to know the key to eternal life, Jesus said: "Sell all that you have and distribute to the poor, . . . and come, follow me" (Luke 18:22).

Contrasting the rich man's rejection was the conversion of Zacchaeus. His conversion led to acts of economic sharing, as well as to the correction of economic injustice: "Behold, Lord, the half of my goods I give to the poor; and if I have defrauded any one of anything, I restore it fourfold." To which Jesus replied: "Today salvation has come to this house" (Luke 19:1-10).

One final indication of the importance of food appeared in the closing days of Jesus' ministry. On the road to Emmaus, He broke bread with two men (Luke 24:13-15). Only with the sharing of food did they know the risen Lord (Luke 24:31).

Again and again, the breaking of bread is tied with love for one another. Sharing bread and sharing hospitality are signs of the Christian community. Notice that in the feeding of the 5,000 (Luke 9:10-17), the Last Supper (Luke 22:14-20), and the experience on the road to Emmaus (Luke 24:13-35), the breaking of bread and the revelation of Who Jesus really is are bound together. Could it be that the world knows who we are by how we respond to the hungry?

Intrachurch aid

The early Christian church knew well about the life and teachings of Jesus. The first Christians tried to follow in His footsteps. They maintained Jesus' concern about breaking bread and sharing hospitality. They retained a strong sense of mutual responsibility for one another. The very nature of the first Christian community copied the pattern of economic sharing which Jesus introduced.

At Pentecost, 3,000 people joined the apostles through the experience of conversion (Acts 2:41-42). This new community in Jerusalem "had all things in common; and they sold their possessions and goods and distributed them to all, as any had need" (Acts 2:44-45). It was an economic community where everyone "partook of food with glad and generous hearts" (Acts 2:46). In fact, the early Christians shared to such an extent that "there was not a needy person among them" (Acts 4:34), a remarkable feat, considering the widespread poverty.

However, not everyone in the early community was poor. A few members were wealthy. And they occasionally sold property with the proceeds being distributed "to each as any had need" (Acts 4:34-35).

Two experiences disclosed more about the true nature of this new economic community. In the first story, Barnabas "sold a field which belonged to him, and brought the money and laid it at the apostles' feet" (Acts 4:36-37). In the second story, Ananias and Sapphira sold property but lied about the price, only to suffer the consequences (Acts 5:1-11). Genuine economic sharing was held up as the model to follow, while deceptive generosity was rejected.

Interchurch Aid

Not only did Christians within the same church share, but churches shared with one another. Aid between churches was common.

The first example of aid between churches took place during the reign of Claudius Caesar. Upon hearing of a hunger crisis in Judea, the Christians in Antioch readily responded. They "determined, every one according to his ability, to send relief to the brethren who lived in Judea; and they did so, sending it to the elders by the hand of Barnabas and Saul" (Acts 11:29-30).

Another example of a hunger relief expedition was the Jerusalem offering. Paul devoted a great deal of time to the gathering of donations from among the Gentile Christian churches for the poor in the Jerusalem church (Gal. 2:10). His goal was to feed the hungry, meeting human needs and making peace within the church.

Writing to the Christians in Rome, Paul shared more information about his hunger offering (Rom. 15:22-33). He wrote that the Christians in Macedonia and Achaia had already made "some contribution for the poor among the saints at Jerusalem" (Rom. 15:26). Their contributions grew out of a sense of fellowship. The Jewish Christians had shared with the Gentile Christians the message of Jesus Christ. Now the Gentile Christians were pleased to share their material blessings with the Jewish Christians (Rom. 15:27). This mission was so important that Paul postponed his long-desired missions trip to Rome on the way to Spain (Rom. 15:25). Bringing about reconciliation within the church was crucial.

The words and actions of Jesus, plus the examples of intrachurch and interchurch hunger aid, tell us how important caring for the hungry is. Jesus expresses concern for the total person. He calls His followers to exercise similar concern. The actions of the early church show that Jesus' call was heard and followed.

What are some biblical principles in a hungry world?

From the Bible, we can draw principles which guide involvement in today's world. These principles direct Christians to set the banquet table, but leave the details about how to set the table to us. We know that God wants justice to "roll down like waters and righteousness like a mighty stream" (Amos 5:24), yet God leaves the building of the irrigation system to us.

Little likelihood exists that American society, for example, could literally reinstate the law of gleaning. America is no longer an agrarian society. Nevertheless, gleaning offers a model which can be used in harvesting edible food from farm fields and grocery stores (see the chapter entitled "What Shall We Do About Hunger?" for the discussion on gleaning).

Art Simon, executive director of Bread for the World, points out that "there is a clear biblical word regarding the obligation of a country such as ours to see that children do not go hungry. We do not, however, have a clear biblical word telling us that food stamps or the WIC program (nutrition program for women, infants, and children) is the way to feed them."[5] Thus, Christians must use their intelligence to translate the biblical message into tangible programs.

This exercise can be an act of loving God. Loving God with all our minds means that we use our intelligence and common sense to do what God wants. Love of God does not mean that we shut down our minds. Instead, calculating analysis, bold planning, and careful implementation reveal love for God.

Here are just a few biblical principles which give Christians a sense of direction. First, God's desire is that poverty and hunger not exist. Yet, the sinful nature of humanity and social evil means that human suffering is part of the fabric of fallen creation. Only with a thorough understanding of the desire of God against the backdrop of human brokenness can we appreciate fully the task before us.

Second, God's covenant people have a special responsibility to offer a hand of help with the right attitude to the hungry. God is more concerned about the covenant community caring for the needy than practicing self-serving, shallow religion. Right worship and right action are inseparable.

Third, we care for the hungry in a variety of ways. One is through acts of charity, such as what the church in Antioch did for the church in Jerusalem (Acts 11:27-30). Another way is through the pursuit of justice, removing barriers which keep people poor and building bridges which lead to opportunities. The story of Zacchaeus, for example, tells us that he had obtained his wealth through taxation at the expense of the poor and that he pursued justice when he restored fourfold what he had obtained wrongly. When we read the prophets, we see that they called for fairness in the marketplace.

A third way is through programs which offer a hand up to self-reliance. Such is the case with Moses' instructions to slaveholders when they freed slaves during the sabbatical year: "You shall open your hand to him, and lend him sufficient for his need" (Deut. 15:8).

[1]John Cheyne, "A.D. 2000: A Formidable Challenge to Christian Witness and Ministry," *Light*, August/September 1987, 1, 3.

[2]Jack Nelson, *Hunger for Justice: The Politics of Food and Faith* (Maryknoll, New York: Orbis Books, 1980), 1.

[3]Wolfgang Stegemann, *The Gospel and the Poor* (Philadelphia: Fortress Press, 1984), 17.

[4]Ibid., 3.

[5]Art Simon, "Art to Art," *Seeds*, August 1987, 23.

3
Africa in crisis

"A biblical famine . . . now, in the twentieth century" was a stunning phrase in an "NBC Nightly News" television report on October 23, 1984, about the hunger crisis in Ethiopia. The news shocked the nation. Even before the newscast ended, a tidal wave of calls washed over NBC. People wanted to know what they could do. Another report was aired the next night. Again, the response was overwhelming. CBS and ABC ran reports the next week, receiving the same staggering response. The African famine became headline news.[1]

From the fall of 1984 through the summer of 1985, the African hunger crisis was a major news story which compelled Americans to respond. Forty-five American rock artists recorded "We Are the World." A 16-hour global rock concert raised pledges of $70 million. A cartoonist for Denver's *Rocky Mountain News* sold his editorial cartoons to raise money for relief. A ten-year-old Maryland schoolgirl sold her prized dollhouse for the homeless refugees.

Among those who responded were Southern Baptists. An anonymous Southern Baptist layman of First Baptist Church, Belfry, Kentucky, gave $100,000 through the Foreign Mission Board to feed the victims of famine. Cecil Staton, pastor of a small North Carolina Baptist church, sparked the collection of a spontaneous hunger offering of $77,428 at the Southern Baptist Convention in 1985. Overall Southern Baptist hunger giving through the Foreign and Home Mission Boards jumped from $5,996,000 in 1983 to $7,166,772 in 1984, and then soared to $11,830,146 in 1985.

Standing as bookends around this flurry of activity were two disturbing facts, however. The African hunger crisis had been developing for almost two years. Hunger experts and relief agencies knew what was happening. They tried to generate news stories. Some secular newspapers covered the crisis, but the electronic news media demonstrated little interest. And the message did not hit home. Not until the general American public saw the starvation on their television screens did they respond.

Second, concern about the crisis withered as quickly as it had sprung up. The television networks and newspapers found other news stories. Hunger contributions dropped dramatically.

Misunderstanding about the nature of the African hunger crisis (and consequently what should be done) was one of the major reasons American interest suddenly faded. Fifteen months after NBC's first report, 17 to 19 million Africans, or about 60 percent of the number in 1985, still faced critical food shortages. In the fall of 1987 an estimated 13 million people in Angola, Ethiopia, Mozambique, and the Sudan were in jeopardy of a food deficit. Thirty percent of all African children were still chronically malnourished. Hunger had not disappeared from the second largest continent in the world.

We misunderstood the crisis for two primary reasons. We defined hunger as the matchstick-looking child. We defined hunger solely as starvation, excluding chronic malnutrition. And, we believed the cause of the crisis was primarily the lack of rain. The equation was simple: If drought caused famine, then rain would end the famine. So we prayed for rain. When reports of rain appeared, we assumed that the crisis had ended. We then turned to other problems. A better understanding of the food crisis would have resulted in a different response.

World hunger is a worldwide problem. In order to explore it more thoroughly, spotlighting one region is instructive. And what part of the world deserves more concentrated focus than Africa? Many of the causes of and cures for hunger in Africa apply elsewhere in the world. An understanding of these factors enables us better to understand hunger around the world.

Africa's hunger crisis: the causes

The African hunger crisis is multidimensional. It denies the temptation of singular answers. It is not simply the lack of rain or overpopulation. It is not just a matter of poor economic choices.

It is a complex crisis of interwoven factors stretching across many decades.

Colonialism

The politics of colonialism provides a beginning point to understanding the African hunger crisis. When the European colonial powers haphazardly carved up Africa a century ago, they ignored African kingdoms, tribal boundaries, linguistical groupings, social relationships, and other factors. They divided some ethnic groups while forcing others together. The unification of tribes with ancient conflictual relationships and stubborn ethnic loyalties offered no basis upon which to build modern nation-states. The geopolitically insensitive European boundaries doomed Africa to intense struggles for national unity.

The arrival of independence in the early 1960s forced the relatively new nations to stand upon their own feet. Some colonial powers had worked to prepare sub-Saharan Africa for independence. Others had not. Many European colonial powers had taken from the continent and then left it empty-handed and unprepared for independence.

For example, when the Portuguese abandoned Mozambique, they sabotaged industrial equipment, ripped out phone lines, and drove tractors into the sea. A nation of 10 million people had only 12 university graduates to run the government. After hundreds of years of colonial rule, only 1 out of every 20 Mozambicans could read or write. When the Belgians gave Zaire independence, a nation roughly the size of the US east of the Mississippi was left with only 16 college graduates to manage the nation.

The lack of colonial investment in developing nations plus the patchwork nature of African boundaries made political instability commonplace, a plague which in turn discouraged economic development. Since it usually was the only institution able to hold nations together, the military became a key to nationhood. Paradoxically, it also became a key factor in the hunger crisis.

War and military spending

At the height of the 1984-85 African famine, wars raged in a number of the 28 nations facing a problem of hunger. Ethiopia, Sudan, Chad, Angola, and Mozambique were engaged in civil wars—wars which affected these nations and their surrounding neighbors. The fighting caused hunger through the disruption of farming, the destruction of marketing facilities, and the decline of economic growth.

Additionally, these wars displaced farmers, as well as others. For example, the Central African Republic was flooded with tens of thousands of refugees fleeing from the strife in Chad. Zaire hosted 280,000 refugees from Angola; Zambia had 100,000 displaced Angolans. Zimbabwe became an escape valve for Mozambicans. Not surprisingly, a massive number of Africans became refugees.

Another dimension of the role of the military has been the drain of limited resources away from human needs. In recent years many African nations have spent an alarming amount on the military. Ethiopia reportedly spends 42 percent of its budget for the military, while Mali spends 21 percent. Perhaps an even greater rationale for enormous military expenditures is the need for military dictatorships to maintain strong and happy armies. Consequently, governments have less revenue to spend on agricultural development, health care, education, and economic growth. Human needs give way to political power considerations.

A revealing statistic is that Africa's military spending rose almost 7 percent each year during the 1970s, while its economic growth hovered around the 1 percentile mark. Could it be that such a rate of military spending slowed down the growth of African economies? Could it be that the import of arms adversely affected national development, further impoverishing nations?

Economics

The economic situation across most of Africa is bleak. Economic stagnation and inadequate production plague many nations. Exceptions are few and far between. What Swaziland, Rwanda, Ivory Coast, and Malawi have accomplished in the way of economic health is rare.

As with political instability, the colonial legacy adversely affected the continent's agricultural economy, setting in place a system which would not fill empty stomachs. The colonial powers shifted the most fertile land from producing food crops to producing nonfood crops—crops for export such as cotton, tobacco, rubber, coffee, and cocoa. These cash crops generated income for the colonial powers. When independence came, however, many of the African nations retained the pattern of cash crops. The cash crops gave these new nations export earnings with which to support industrial development.

The eventual consequence was twofold. First, Africa's self-sufficiency in food crops gave way to an unnecessary dependency on imported grain.[2] In 1970, Africa imported little food from abroad. By 1984 the picture had changed dramatically. Twenty-four million tons of grain were being imported. A food-producing continent had become a continent dependent on food grown elsewhere.

A second consequence concerned the breakdown of much of Africa's environment. Since cash crops were grown on the most fertile land, food crops were forced onto second-rate land. Food production soon fell. The fragile soil was unable to support crops year after year. When farmland failed, farmers searched for new cropland. In the process, they left the overcultivated land barren and cut down more and more forests, stripping away the natural environment which held moisture in the soil and retarded soil erosion. This ecological deterioration dealt another blow to already frail economies.

Another contributor to the decline in food production has been the nature of government price controls. Many African governments have kept food prices low, encouraging the growth of crops for export and discouraging the growth of grain for domestic consumption. Low food prices keep urban populations happy. With 30 percent of all Africans living in cities, many of whom are impoverished, high food prices can spark riots and even revolts. Governments know that national stability depends on keeping city dwellers satisfied. Cheap food, however, has a negative side. It takes away the incentive for farmers to grow food for sale.

The global economy has also impacted Africa. A sevenfold increase in oil prices and a drop in commodity prices has battered national economies. Annual economic growth in Africa has plummeted from a peak of 6 percent in 1974 to less than 2 percent in 1982. Few signs indicate that this trend will reverse.

Additionally, the international debt burdens Africa's economy. According to a report of the Committee on African Development Strategies, "on the average, more than half of all export earnings are now required to service foreign loans; for some countries, debt service actually exceeds export earnings."[3] Africa's debt, acquired when banks encouraged lending, keeps it from investing scarce resources in productive enterprises which could lead to self-sufficiency and economic growth.

Population

Many people believe hunger results from overpopulation: too many children are born into a world with too little food. The only way to increase the food supply is to decrease the birthrate. Such a belief is understandable, especially in Africa where population growth outstrips food production.

Africa's population growth rate has increased from 2.4 percent in the 1960s to 3.2 percent in the 1980s, compared to less than 1 percent in the United States, 1 percent in China, and 2.3 percent in Latin America. At the present rate of growth, the sub-Saharan population promises to double by year 2000.

A key question here is: what causes Africa's population boom? Several answers are often given. One is a value system which causes women to fear barrenness and desire the prestige of large families. On the male side of the equation, numerous children are seen as a sign of potency. Cultural factors influence the growth rate.

Another answer is that children are a source of economic security. Children provide farm labor, as well as insurance against economic hard times in old age. The high infant and childhood mortality rates, sometimes 50 times higher than that in the United States, encourage women to have many pregnancies, hoping some children survive to adulthood to guard against threats to old age.

A second critical question concerns the impact of population on hunger. Clearly, tremendous population growth places stress on food production, the environment, and the economy. It also threatens government stability.

But does population growth cause hunger? Experts disagree on the answer. Frances Moore Lappé and Joseph Collins make an interesting observation: "China has only half the cropland per person as India, yet Indians suffer widespread and severe hunger while Chinese do not. . . . Costa Rica, with less than half of Honduras' cropped acres per person, boasts a life expectancy—one indicator of nutrition—14 years longer than that of Honduras and close to that of the Western industrial countries."[4] They suggest that what population growth and hunger share in common is poverty—poverty stimulates population growth and causes hunger.

Environment

Environmental conditions across much of Africa are harsh. The arid climate, the weak soil, and the constant erosion make food production most difficult. The commonplace nature of drought compounds the problem.

Many people recognize that the lack of rain contributes to hunger. Few people know why "since 1967 . . . Africa has seen 17 straight years of below-average rainfall . . . and the last two years have been more than 40 percent short."[5] Some believe drought occurs in cycles. Others think human activities such as deforestation are actually pulling the Sahara Desert southward. What is clear is that areas which once produced food are now too arid to farm. In the Sahel region alone, the desert has swallowed an area the size of Austria and France in half a century.

As mentioned under the section on economics, farmers have overcultivated the land and destroyed woodland in search of new cropland. Similarly, herdsmen have overgrazed pastures, and both activities have increased soil erosion. The loss of topsoil makes food production even more difficult, which may account for declining crop yields.

Compounding the negative side effects of farming and ranching practices is the nature of energy consumption. In Sahel, between 80 and 90 percent of the energy consumed comes from burning firewood. Even oil-rich Nigeria gets 80 percent of its energy needs from firewood. And most of this wood is used in cooking!

Indeed, the need for cooking fuel has stripped many cities of the forests which once surrounded them. "No forests remain within 70 kilometers [44 miles] of Niamey, the capital of Niger, or of Ouagadougou, the capital of Burkina Faso."[6] To make the problem even worse, trees are not being replanted. Twenty-nine trees are chopped down for every 1 planted. Africa is rapidly losing its forests.

The destruction of trees to meet the energy needs of a rapidly expanding population and the demands of farmers contributes to the breakdown of the environment. Environmental mismanagement tears down the natural barriers to wind and soil erosion and uproots the very source which holds moisture in the soil. Like crashing billiards, one ball sets another ball in motion. Each factor affects another.

Foreign aid

Foreign aid is a hotly debated topic. Many Americans believe foreign aid is a giveaway program that ought to be cut back or stopped altogether. Others contend foreign aid desperately needs reform. Few verbalize satisfaction with it.

An increasing number of people assert that foreign aid adds to Africa's other problems. Too often it has been used to build symbols of progress such as airports, dams, shipping ports, hotels, roads, and conference centers. Such projects frequently end up costing too much for African governments to support. Over time these projects become run-down or abandoned. Today Africa is littered with these so-called cathedrals in the desert, constant reminders of the failure of foreign aid and evidence that it does not go to help the typical African farmer become self-reliant or the small-scale entrepreneur expand her business.

Lloyd Timberlake, author of the award winning book entitled *Africa in Crisis,* notes how foreign aid to Sahel was spent in the early 1980s. Thirty-five percent went to food aid and to help with balance of payments. Thirty percent went into transportation, telecommunications, health, and education projects. Another 30 percent was invested in projects such as irrigated and rainfed cash crops. Only 4 percent went to farmers growing food for consumption.[7]

US Secretary of State George Shultz acknowledged the misguided side of foreign aid. "Some of our aid," he said, "has been counterproductive, contributing to dependence rather than self-reliance, stagnation rather than growth."[8]

Aside from the misguided dimension of foreign aid is the issue of why foreign aid is even offered. A brief look at the nature of US foreign aid is instructive. When the Food for Peace program, part of US foreign aid, was begun in 1954, it had two purposes: to keep American agricultural surpluses from depressing the domestic market prices and to create future markets for agricultural products. Only later was the program changed to encourage economic development in poor countries and to help hungry people.

Humanitarian objectives, however, are only one dimension of foreign aid. The US has used foreign aid to encourage cooperation, to secure access to strategic resources, and to promote strategic interests. In 1985, for example, three Central American nations received almost four times more US food aid per capita than the famine-stricken region of sub-Saharan Africa.

Foreign aid often serves economic objectives. Such is the case when the donor nation requires the recipient nation to purchase goods, equipment, and expertise from itself, even though the items could be purchased more cheaply elsewhere. In 1980, for example, three out of every four dollars in the US Agency for International Development (AID) budget went to purchase products and services in the US. According to Frances Moore Lappé and Joseph Collins, "In fiscal year 1984, 20 US corporations and universities received over $159 million in AID funds, equal to almost half of US development assistance to sub-Saharan Africa that year."[9]

Misguided foreign aid projects do little to alleviate poverty. Rather than help, foreign aid sometimes hurts the people in the recipient nation. What is needed is for foreign aid to offer impoverished nations a hand up to self-reliance.

Africa's hunger crisis: cures

Few people claim to know all the answers to Africa's crisis. Because previous strategies have worked marginally, analyzing the problem is easier than finding the solutions. The best people can do is to suggest a series of partial answers, hoping that some of the strategies for alleviating hunger will actually work.

Study

Perhaps one of the most important first steps American Christians can take to respond to Africa's hunger crisis is to learn more about it. Africa has been called the Dark Continent. But the real dark continent may be America where most United States citizens remain in the dark about most of the world, especially African nations. We know virtually nothing about most of the 42 sub-Saharan states, a sad commentary about a nation where educational institutions flourish.

Our ignorance is surprising, considering that for 137 years Southern Baptists have sent missionaries to Africa. In 1988 the Foreign Mission Board had 880 career missionaries in 34 African nations and spent $28 million there to do missions. Southern Baptist heritage coupled with the Convention's investment of financial and human resources should be motivation enough to learn more about this continent. Furthermore, the spiraling growth of Christianity in Africa ought to compel Southern Baptists to expand their level of awareness.

Besides tracking the growth of missions work, understanding

more about Africa would enable Christians to better influence governmental policymakers and elected officials. Knowledge can be used to influence the public debate, creating a climate which favors policies designed to empower the poor through programs leading out of poverty to self-reliance. Informed opinions can leaven the entire national loaf.

Knowledge also enables Christians to ask pointed questions about such issues as foreign aid. For example, why does US AID not have a full-time irrigation specialist at its headquarters in Washington, D.C., or in regional offices in Africa? Or why does so little aid go to African women, who do between 60 and 80 percent of the farm labor? Asking the right questions may increase the likelihood that government programs will get on the right path.

Before charging helter-skelter into the public square with our solutions, however, we need to study the issue. The more we learn, the more complex we will find the problem and the more elusive we will find the answer. Neither experience, however, should keep Christians from acting. We must support programs we think will work, without confusing human opinions with divine answers.

Economics

As is true in the United States and around the world, poverty is a major cause of hunger. The fact that Africa is the poorest continent on the globe should prevent Christians from being surprised about its widespread hunger. And if poverty causes hunger, then we know that one way to reduce hunger, and perhaps to slow the rate of population growth, is through economic development.

Both internal and external forces can encourage economic development. Within the continent, African nations must focus greater attention on the agricultural sector. More governmental resources must be devoted to develop rural Africa. Furthermore, governments must provide greater incentives to boost food production, as well as cash crop production. One way to encourage the former idea is through a less tightly controlled market system.

Carl Eicher, a professor of agricultural economics at Michigan State University, writes that "in terms of agricultural production goals, capitalism has proven to be a more reliable strategy than socialism at this stage of Africa's economic history. After 25 years of independence, there are no models of agrarian socialism in Africa that have produced a reliable agricultural surplus."[10] However, Eicher warns that neither the ideology of capitalism nor socialism promise to bring about agricultural surpluses.

Outside the continent, developed nations must improve the nature of their foreign aid. Foreign aid ought to encourage economic development among the poor, not just to build symbols of progress or to stimulate the donor nation's economy. Additionally, foreign aid research ought to focus on small-scale agricultural projects leading to self-sufficiency.

A study of US AID's budget for Africa indicates that in 1985 only 4.3 percent of its funding was for women-specific projects, and only 4 of the 45 agricultural projects were designed to benefit women. Considering the fact that women do between 60 and 80 percent of the continent's farm work and manage 30 percent of the farms, these figures are a shocking illustration of misguided aid.

Imagine what could be accomplished if more US foreign aid had to go to women farmers, more American female agriculturalists were assigned to train African women, and more AID officials were women. Foreign aid might enable the primary food producers to produce more food.

Women in general and the poor in particular need to be targets of foreign aid. Unfortunately, they have not been on the receiving end of development aid. Fortunately, a relatively new strategy has been introduced to help the poor help themselves. It is called micro-enterprise.[11]

Micro-enterprise credit is designed for the poor to get extremely small bank loans for farming and home industries. Previously the poor have not had access to bank loans. With the micro-enterprise system, banks go to the impoverished, offering loans ranging from $1 to $200. Collateral is no longer a prerequisite for getting a loan. Instead, borrowers are placed in groups of five people from their own villages which generates peer pressure for repayment. This strategy has worked so well for the Grameen Bank in Bangladesh that it boasts a repayment rate of 98 percent![12]

If US foreign aid would go into projects such as micro-enterprises, US citizens would feel better about supporting more foreign aid and would be assured that their government was acting responsibly to reduce hunger. Christian citizens may play an important role in encouraging policies offering a hand up to self-reliance. We can urge our elected representatives to increase funding for organizations such as the International Fund for Agricultural Development and the African Development Foundation which promote micro-enterprise strategies.

Another aspect of foreign aid concerns the international debt. With 50 to 60 percent of its export earnings going to service debt repayment, African nations have few resources to pursue development. Most people recognize that the debt crisis causes hunger. Few know what should be done to eliminate a factor which stifles economic growth.

A number of proposals have been made. One solution is for developed nations and international financial institutions to reschedule the debt with no interest, as was done for Indonesia in 1970. Another suggestion is for debts to be forgiven. A moratorium on debt repayment for ten years is another answer. Finally, nations could increase their foreign aid to service the debt, to introduce better management skills, and to reduce the need for borrowing.

Although Africa's total debt is small when compared to that of Latin America, it is much heavier, for African economies are weaker. Nevertheless, resolving the international debt crisis is an international necessity. Whatever the final solution is for the Third-World debt, it must be worked out quickly to avert an even greater worldwide economic crisis.

Green revolution

For much of the world the development of stronger and more productive kinds of crops, called the green revolution, begun 20 years ago, has been heralded as an agricultural success. It has been considered one of the most successful international efforts since the Marshall Plan rebuilt Europe. Today India has grain reserves, while Indonesia exports rice. Nevertheless, both nations still have widespread poverty. The green revolution has successfully increased the production of certain food crops. It has not ended hunger.

On the African scene the green revolution has not increased food production for two reasons. First, the green revolution has concentrated its research on wheat and rice, which are not foods eaten across most of Africa. Millet, sorghum, cassava, and yams are the subsistence crops for most Africans, yet they have received little research attention. Second, the green revolution requires lots of rich soil and water, neither of which exist in abundance in Africa.

Today, greater research attention is being paid to the green revolution in Africa. A new breed of cassava, a root crop, is reportedly spreading among Nigerian farmers. It doubles the yield without chemical fertilizers and with less labor. In Sudan, a new variety of sorghum has been developed which produces 150 percent more than the traditional strain. Such examples suggest that Africa can successfully produce more food crops.

Part of the green revolution must include care for the environment, as well as small-scale, low-cost technological advances. Undoubtedly, Africa must begin a massive reforestation effort. But without greater foreign assistance, this will not likely succeed.

Some environmental projects do offer hope. One of the best known is the 230 miles of double-row windbreak trees in the Majjia Valley of Niger. Begun in 1974 by CARE, this innovative project conserves the soil, provides villagers with firewood, and may be the reason why area grain yields have increased by 23 percent. The project is an excellent example of where foreign assistance and hands-on involvement of local villagers protect the environment and combat hunger.

Another part of the equation is low-cost technological innovations. Several examples stand out here. One is the introduction in Ethiopia of a newly designed animal yoke which allows one oxen, rather than two, to pull a plow. A second is a simple, inexpensive mud stove in Burkina Faso. Traditionally, food has been cooked over an open fire which wastes energy. The mud stove, on the other hand, consumes less energy, reducing the number of sticks burned from five to one. Such technological advances improve the livelihood of the poor as they guard the environment.

The green revolution designed for poor farmers and small-scale, low-cost projects are not the total answer to Africa's hunger crisis. They do offer, however, a better alternative than previous efforts. They do help the poor to help themselves.

Military spending

Military spending is a spin-off of the political instability resulting from the heritage of colonialism. The shortsightedness, greed, and national arrogance of the past press upon the present, even a century later. The injustices of the past cannot be erased.

But they can be remembered. In remembering them, we can check the temptation to claim that we have all the answers. And American Christians do not have all the answers, especially concerning what can be done about military spending. The lack of absolute certainty, however, does not free Christians from acting.

A widespread belief is that without political stability, solid economic growth remains elusive. The key then is encouraging programs leading to political stability. One way to accomplish this goal is to urge the United States, Soviet Union, European nations, China, and Israel to stop pushing arms into Africa. Military hardware sales do not ensure security. Indeed, they may introduce even more insecurity.

All the arms-producing nations work hard at promoting sales to other nations. It stimulates their own economies, while furthering their nation's foreign policy. The US, for example, has expanded military sales to Africa to accomplish numerous objectives. US sales have spiraled upward 150 percent since 1981, and the number of nations receiving military aid has increased from 19 to 36 states. Such a beehive of activity may counter Soviet actions. Nevertheless, pushing arms into Africa does little for African economic well-being.

What is needed is for American Christians to encourage their government to work on an international level to discourage arms sales in Africa. Working for peace is one way to work against hunger. Peacemaking can come in the form of antihunger efforts.

[1]Peter J Boyer, "Famine in Ethiopia: The TV Accident that Exploded," *Seeds*, April 1985, 24-27.

[2]For another opinion on the issue of food crops versus cash crops, see Paul Harrison, *The Greening of Africa: Breaking Through in the Battle for Land Food* (New York: Penguin Books, 1987).

[3]Robert J. Berg and Jennifer Seymour Whitaker, eds., Report of the Committee on African Development Strategies, *Strategies for African Development* (Berkeley: University of California Press, 1986), 573.

[4]Frances Moore Lappé and Joseph Collins, *World Hunger: Twelve Myths* (New York: Grove Press, Inc., 1986), 23-24.

[5]Lester R. Brown and Edward C. Wolf, *Reversing Africa's Decline*, World Watch Paper 65 (June 1985): 20.

[6]Lester R. Brown and Jodi Jacobson,"Assessing the Future of Urbanization," Linda Stankel, ed., *State of the World 1987* (New York: W. W. Norton and Company, 1987), 43.

[7]Lloyd Timberlake, *Africa in Crisis: The Causes, the Cures of Environmental Bankruptcy* (Washington, D.C.: Earthscan, 1985), 38.

[8]George Shultz, "The Challenge of African Economic Reform," January 8, 1987, United States Department of State, Current Policy No. 907, 2.

[9]Lappé and Collins, *World Hunger,* 110.

[10]Carl K. Eicher, "Strategy in Issues in Combatting Hunger and Poverty in Africa," Robert S.Berg and Jennifer Seymour Whitaker, eds. (Berkeley: University of California Press, 1986), 250.

[11]Larry Hollar, "The Enterprising Poor," *Bread,* Spring 1987, 7-10.

[12]Patricia Ayres and Juana Rodriguez, "Working Together on Hunger Needs in Bangladesh," *Royal Service,* February 1988, 7.

4
Hunger on the home front

America has a hunger problem.

Fifteen nationwide studies in the past several years all reached similar conclusions: The United States has a large number of people who regularly experience hunger. It is not the kind of hunger associated with mass starvation in Third-World countries. It is the kind of grinding hunger which dulls the ability of children to learn in school, reduces the productivity of adults, and weakens the immune system of the elderly. It is the kind of hunger which is often an unseen problem whose well-recognized side effects are susceptibility to disease, low-birth-weight infants, and infant mortality.

Who are the hungry Americans?

According to an intense ten-month study by physicians and public health experts who traveled back roads, opened refrigerators, and studied documents, an estimated 20 million Americans "may be hungry at least some period of time each month."[1]

The task force concluded that "the problem of hunger in the United States is now more widespread and serious than at any time in the last ten to fifteen years."[2]

This study, entitled *Hunger in America: The Growing Epidemic,* cited an array of evidence to support its conclusions. Health clinics in poor communities were reporting cases of kwashiorkor and marasmus, two diseases of advanced malnutrition usually associated with the Third World. Second Harvest, an umbrella organization of food banks, had a 700 percent increase in food distribution since 1980. And the infant mortality rate was leveling off instead of declining like that of other industrial nations. The report painted a bleak portrait of the poor in America.

Beyond all the reports, medical evidence of malnutrition, and the statistics are the real people—people like Pat Jones, Effie Alsop, Letta Casey, and John Hosmer. Each knows hunger first-hand. Each represents a different face of hunger in a land of plenty.

When physicians investigating hunger visited Pat Jones's home in Montgomery, Alabama, they found that her refrigerator contained only three eggs, one slice of cheese, and a water jug. Her three-year-old son had not had milk to drink in three weeks. The morning the physicians arrived, he had had the last of the cereal with water.[3]

At the other end of the age spectrum was Effie Alsop. Interviewed in her southern Missouri home, this 86-year-old woman told a physician: "I get hungry when food is in the house, but when I don't have any, I'm not hungry. Isn't that funny, doctor?"[4]

Testifying in 1985 before the Select Committee on Hunger of the US House of Representatives, Letta Casey, a 38-year-old single parent of two boys, told about poverty in Roses Creek Hollow, Tennessee. She testified that she could not feed her family on government food stamps and expressed thanks for the federal school breakfast and lunch programs.

"When school started [in September]," she said, "I was one of the happiest people in the world because I knew the boys was gonna eat better than I was."[5]

The same year that Letta Casey talked about hunger in rural Appalachia, John Hosmer told about hunger in Columbus, Ohio. Economic hard times had left his family unemployed, forcing them to move across the country looking for work. For a while, John, his wife, and their two sons lived in their old blue Chevy Malibu. Once he even gave blood to get eight dollars for food.[6]

Hunger in America is real. But policymakers, politicians, and antihunger advocates cannot agree on the extent of the problem because the nation lacks a "hunger index." The federal government can measure all sorts of economic indicators. As of yet, however, the nation cannot measure definitively the nutritional status of its citizens.

Representative Mickey Leland (D-Tex.), chairman of the House Select Committee on Hunger, has said, "At present we do not know how many hungry or malnourished people there are in the United States. . . . [T]here is no national data. We should establish a national system of nutrition monitoring."[7]

The lack of a hunger index means that other data is used to determine need. Emergency food center surveys, investigative news stories, medical reports, and studies by religious organizations contribute insight into the problem. Government statistics related to low birth weights, the infant mortality rate, poverty figures, unemployment statistics, and the number of recipients of food stamps and other welfare programs are used to measure hunger.

Through the years citizens concerned about hunger have called for a nutritional monitoring system. Not until June of 1986, however, did the US House of Representatives pass a bill establishing a national hunger watch program. If the Senate passes a similar bill, future Americans will have definitive, quantitative proof about the extent of hunger.

Until this system is in place, people concerned about hunger will continue to operate with the correct assumption that the poor are those most at risk to hunger. What poverty does is to put people in a situation of having to decide between necessities such as food and shelter. The poor must decide between purchasing food or paying the rent. They must choose between buying milk or medicine. Frequently they decide to go without food, and the consequence is hunger. Nancy Amidei, a commentator on National Public Radio, perceptively notes that "hunger goes with poverty."[8]

In order to get a better picture of those most at risk to hunger, it is necessary to isolate certain groups. Children, senior citizens, the homeless, working people, and rural Americans are just a few of the groups discussed. Others who face mealtimes as tough times include migrant workers and refugees.

The Children

Children are the poorest Americans. Thirteen million children live in poverty. The younger the child, the greater is the chance that the child lives in poverty. Twenty-four percent of American children under 6 are poor, compared to 20 percent for children 6 to 17 years of age. According to Marian Wright Edleman, a Baptist and president of the Children's Defense Fund, a profamily organization, "poverty takes one American child's life every fifty-three minutes. More American children die each year from poverty than from traffic fatalities and suicide combined."[9]

The shocking plight of children is a recent historical development. "In 1974, children replaced the elderly as the poorest age group in the United States," writes Barbara Howell, an issue analyst for Bread for the World. "The United States is the only industrialized nation in the world where children comprise the largest segment of the poverty population."[10]

One of the most devastating impacts of poverty is the infant mortality rate (IMR). The IMR measures deaths to children under 1 year of age per 1,000 live births and is linked to low birth weights. In fact, two thirds of infant deaths are associated with low birth weights. Babies who weigh 5.5 pounds or less are 40 times more likely to die in the first month than normal weight babies and are twice as likely to suffer severe handicaps such as deafness, blindness, or mental retardation.

Although unanimous agreement about the cause of low birth weights does not prevail among health experts, general agreement exists that inadequate prenatal care and poor nutrition contribute to low birth weights. Not surprisingly, the failure to seek medical care and eat the right food is greatest among poor pregnant women.

The Children's Defense Fund issued a report in 1987 which found that the United States ranked last among 20 industrialized nations in terms of the IMR. Almost 11 babies out of every 1,000 born in the US die before their first birthday, compared to 10 in the United Kingdom, 9 in France, 7 in Sweden, and 6 in Japan. Between 1950 and 1955 and 1980 and 1985, Japan lowered its infant mortality rate from 51 to 6, while the US dropped its rate from 28 to 11.

Figures on the US show that nine of the ten states with the highest IMR are located in the South: South Carolina (14.7), Mississippi (14.4), Alabama (12.9), Georgia (12.9), North Carolina (12.4), Virginia (12.1), Louisiana (12.1), and Tennessee (11.8). Other southern states with high rates include Kentucky (11.5), Arkansas (10.9), Florida (10.8), Oklahoma (10.8), Texas (10.5), and Missouri (10.4).

Regardless of where American infants live, black babies are almost twice as likely to die as white babies. The status of black infants is put in stark terms with the statistic that "a black infant born within five miles of the White House in our nation's capital is more likely to die in the first year of life than an infant born in third world countries like Trinidad and Tobago or Costa Rica."[11]

In Humphreys County, located in the Mississippi Delta and called the Catfish Capital of the World, the infant deaths are almost 42 per 1,000, a rate higher than the nations of Malaysia and Sri Lanka. The high rate in the Delta counties results from a toxic blend of poverty and teenage pregnancy. Poor teenagers often become pregnant out of wedlock; pregnant teenagers often become trapped in poverty. The cycle is vicious, and deadly.

Larry Brown, chairman of the Harvard School of Public Health, believes: "Whatever the circumstances of an infant's gestation and birth, the child once born is at considerable risk if adequate nutrition is lacking. The human brain develops most rapidly from conception until about the age of three. During those years brain function can be impaired by nutritional deprivation."[12] Other health risks, according to Brown, are below-average height and weight growth, as well as vulnerability to environmental toxins.

Another indication of the childhood risk to hunger is the large number of eligible people, but low level of participation in the Special Supplemental Food Program for Women, Infants and Children (WIC). WIC provides packages of nutritious foods to pregnant women, nursing mothers, and children under age five. These packages of milk, cheese, eggs, juice, infant formula, and peanut butter improve the likelihood of healthier mothers and babies, a necessary step toward reduction of the infant mortality rate. Furthermore, several studies have indicated that WIC saves money. For every one dollar spent on WIC, an estimated three dollars can be saved in hospital intensive care costs for low-birth-weight infants with health problems. The effectiveness of WIC is well recognized, yet only 3.3 million out of the 8.4 million people eligible for WIC receive it. Another 5 million women, infants, and children face the threat of hunger.

The elderly

The elderly are another group of Americans often considered at risk to hunger. An estimated 3.3 million, or 12.6 percent, of Americans over the age of 65 have incomes below the poverty line. Recent government statistics indicate that elderly black and Hispanic males have a much great chance of being poor than elderly white males and that elderly women are poorer than elderly men. Furthermore, older Americans living alone are poorer than those living in couples. The most surprising data discloses that rural elderly are poorer than the urban elderly.

A 1984 statewide survey in Texas found that 58 percent of those who received home-delivered meals or meals at churches or centers said that such meals were their "only complete meal of the day." Thirty-four percent said that they would go hungry without these meals.[13] Despite the critical value of these meals, many elderly Texans, as citizens in other states, were not participating in the program. Many did not know they were eligible; others were too proud to participate.

As the nation ages, a greater number of elderly citizens will be at risk to hunger. Additionally, a larger percentage of the poor will be senior citizens. The so-called golden years could easily dim into hard times.

The homeless

One of the most visible groups of hungry people is the homeless. No one knows exactly how many Americans are homeless. The estimates range from as low as 500,000 to as high as 3,000,000. Authorities disagree on the number, but almost everyone recognizes that a growing number of Americans are homeless for a variety of reasons some time every year. They can be seen in downtown libraries, under overpasses, outside post offices, around bus depots, and in old cars with bald tires. They are visible especially in wintertime.

Today between 30 and 40 percent of America's street people are mentally ill. Their disorders include schizophrenia and depression. A study by the US Conference on Mayors estimates that more than 50 percent of the homeless are either mentally ill or alcohol/drug abusers. Of course alcohol/drug abuse may mask psychiatric disorders.

While single men comprise 60 percent of the homeless population, 12 percent are single women, and a startling 28 percent are families. The growing number of homeless women with children and families defies the old stereotypes, outdates the standard facilities, and requires creative alternatives. Women with children and families cannot share facilities with single men. Children need playground space. Many shelters open in the evening and then ask people to leave in the morning, yet families need housing 24 hours a day, not just at night. The new homeless need shelters designed to meet new needs.

The working poor

Another group of Americans at risk to hunger is known as the working poor. An estimated 1.2 million heads of households work full-time, minimum-wage jobs and still live in poverty. In 1986 a man or woman earning $3.35 an hour for 50 weeks a year brings home an income of $6,700, less than the estimated poverty line of $8,934 for a family of three. The result is that a working parent cannot earn enough money to provide basic necessities, one of which is adequate nutrition.

The rural poor

One of the most surprising findings in recent years is that rural America, home for more than 70 percent of all Southern Baptists, may be poorer and hungrier than previously recognized. According to a yearlong study of rural poverty by Public Voice for Food and Health Policy, a consumer research organization, the rural poor "are underfed, undernourished, and in poor health."[14]

The latest statistics indicate that 13.5 million poor people live in rural America, compared to 12.8 million in urban areas of cities with populations of 50,000 or more. The lack of adequate nutrition results in a higher infant mortality rate and lower birth weights. Another indication of chronic undernutrition is the height-for-age indicator. Seven percent of poor rural children are abnormally short compared to 3 percent of nonpoor children.

Addressing poverty in Appalachia, Ronald E. Eller, a Baptist layman and director of the Appalachian Center at the University of Kentucky, has written: "The pain of unemployment and poverty is perhaps nowhere more apparent than in declining health conditions in the region. A recent survey of rural health clinics indicates a rise in nutritional problems, infant mortality, and dietary deficiencies among the elderly. The nutritional status of infants and poor children is declining, and those people who require special diets—such as diabetics and hypertensives—simply can't afford to eat what they should."[15]

For a sizable number of Americans, mealtimes are tough times. Certainly a nation that can spend over $1 million a day storing surplus agricultural bounty and over $300 billion annually on military spending can ensure that all its citizens have access to an adequate diet.

Why are Americans hungry?

Poverty is the chief reason for hunger in America, and poverty is tied to economic hardships. In early 1980 the unemployment rate was 6.2 percent. For the next several years it rose sharply, reaching a peak of 10.8 percent in 1983. The unemployment rate then fell to about 7 percent, still above the level six years earlier. Economic hard times in the so-called rust, oil, and farm belts have put people out of jobs or into jobs which offer little economic security.

Another reason is the weave of the so-called safety net which allows poor people to fall into harder times. One of the holes in the safety net is the problem of mobility. Elderly people may go hungry simply because they lack transportation. Richard Margolis, author of *Risking Old Age in America,* "I have met aged residents . . . who do not collect their food stamps because they cannot afford a 'taxi'—usually a neighbor's pickup truck—to take them to the welfare offices."[16] The disabled and rural residents regularly face this problem. Some state governments require food stamp recipients to pick up their stamps each month rather than allowing them to receive the stamps through the mail. Such hurdles form a barrier to government food assistance.

A second hole in the safety net is the design of the government-sponsored, home-delivered meals. The federal law mandates that this program provide older Americans with one-third of the current daily recommended dietary allowances at least five days a week. The result is that the elderly receive one meal daily and none on weekends.

A third illustration of the weakness of the safety net is the welfare program called Aid to Families with Dependent Children (AFDC). Approximately half of the states, which design many of the eligibility guidelines for welfare, deny benefits if both parents are present in the home. More often than not, what happens is that the father is forced out of the home, leading to family breakup. Such rules are one explanation for why many people view welfare as having an antifamily dimension.

Adding to the problems created by the weave of the safety net is the lack of funding for many antipoverty programs. Although 33 million Americans live in poverty, only 19 million participate in the food stamp program. Only 60 percent of those eligible for food stamps receive them. The lack of funding and the cutoff of outreach funds mean that 40 percent of the eligible people fail to receive public assistance.

Other areas are also inadequately funded. Only 3.3 million out of 8.5 million eligible people receive WIC. More than 3 million poor children do not get school lunches, while almost 12 million do not get school breakfasts.

The lack of funding for these and other programs is disturbing. Even more disturbing are the figures which indicate a great disparity between the rural poor and the urban poor. Public Voice reports that 57 percent of the rural poor, compared to 54 percent of the urban poor, remain unserved by the food stamp program. Translated into per capita numbers, the figures are $222 monthly for the rural dwellers versus $368 for those in cities. An even wider gap exists in AFDC, where monthly per capita figures are $161 for the rural poor compared to $554 for the metropolitan poor.

A fourth explanation for hunger in America is the tax structure. The Children's Defense Fund calculates that in 1979 a family of four just at the poverty line paid less than 2 percent of its earnings in income tax and Social Security, compared to 11 percent in 1986. Although the Tax Reform Act of 1986 corrects this drain on the poor, removing 6.5 million low-income Americans from the tax rolls, it does not make up for all the years of hardship.

Other taxes also restrict the amount of income available to the poor. The recent removal of sales tax on food stamps helps, but a number of states still have a sales tax on food. Alabama, Arkansas, Georgia, Mississippi, North Carolina, South Carolina, and Tennessee all slice the purchasing power of the poor with state sales taxes on food. If the state of Tennessee removed its food tax, for example, 500,000 poor people would have a little more dollar each month for a little more food.

Wasted food also contributes to American hunger. An estimated 60 million tons of food spoils in American farm fields. Grain, fruit, and vegetables simply rot. Additionally, enormous quantities of food are wasted in homes, grocery stores, and restaurants. Wasted food is a problem unique to the United States, yet it also may be a solution to domestic hunger. If just a small portion of the otherwise wasted food could be channeled to the hungry, then a giant step would be taken toward meeting nutritional requirements.

What can we do about hunger in America?

Poverty, and consequently hunger, in America is a deeply entrenched problem. Poverty did not arise overnight, and it will not disappear easily.

The first step toward eliminating hunger in America is to change the public prejudice against the poor. In some ways America's racial prejudice has been replaced by our disdain of poor people. They are often ridiculed and ostracized, when they really deserve the same level of respect from church members and churches that is extended to the wealthy.

Part of changing the public attitude toward the poor is dispelling the popular myth that welfare programs are fraudulent. The Physician Task Force on Hunger in America estimates that fraud, waste, and abuse in programs serving the poor is much less than commonly believed (and probably substantially less than bigger spending programs such as military procurements)."[17] Fraud in the food stamp program, for example, is less than 6 percent.

Fraud is not in the nation's best interest. Neither is bigotry. Eliminating prejudice against the poor would remove the social stigma attached to antipoverty programs, a necessary move in order for some people to feel comfortable with participation in welfare.

A second step is to develop a positive attitude toward children, especially poor children. A hungry child is a child who cannot learn in school. An uneducated child grows into an adult with few skills and little promise of productivity. America needs to view its children as a sacred resource. Like Japan, the US ought to provide free school meals to children, considering it an investment in the future.

A third step is to urge Republicans and Democrats in the US Congress to strengthen antipoverty programs, removing many of the barriers to participation and increasing the level of service available. Programs that have proven track records, such as WIC, need to be expanded. Programs with flaws need to be redesigned with a more human face.

Reforming welfare is certainly a national priority. Welfare programs which contribute to family breakup, perpetuate poverty, and foster dependency are extremely harmful. Welfare programs ought to look after children, the elderly, and the disabled, as well as enable adults to get job training and find jobs.

The US Congress bears much of the responsibility for antipoverty programs, and rightly receives much of the attention. Unfortunately, this results in people overlooking their own state legislatures. Since state legislatures determine many of the welfare guidelines and some of the funding, Christian citizens need to engage in public policy at the state level.

A fourth step is to make the tax system fairer. Removing the sales tax on food is one small but important move toward helping the poor. It would allow the poor to stretch their food dollar just a little farther each month. Of course changing a source of revenue for state governments promises to be controversial.

[1]Physician Task Force on Hunger in America, *Hunger in America: the Growing Epidemic* (Boston: Crane Duplicating Service, 1985), 4.

[2]Ibid., 15.

[3]Ibid., 26.

[4]Ibid., 55.

[5]*Tennessean,* October 23, 1985, 1.

[6]*Washington Post,* June 9, 1985, 1.

[7]Mickey Leland, "To End Hunger in the United States," *Seeds,* June 1986, 11.

[8]Nancy Amidei, "The State of the Union: Hunger on the Home Front," Christian Life Commission Conference, Charlotte, North Carolina, January 1986.

[9]Marian Wright Edleman, "The Poorest Americans Are the Children," *Concern,* January 1987, 4.

[10]Barbara Howell, "Women and Children: Hungry in America," *Bread,* Fall 1986, 7

[11]Children's Defense Fund Press Release, "Nation Slows in Reducing Infant Deaths," February 2, 1987.

[12]J. Larry Brown, "Hunger in the U.S.," *Scientific American,* February 1987, 38.

[13]The State of Texas, Senate Interim Committee on Hunger and Nutrition 1984 Report and Recommendations, *Faces of Hunger in the Shadow of Plenty,* ii.

[14]Jeffrey Shotland, *Rising Poverty, Declining Health: The Nutritional Status of the Rural Poor* (Washington, D.C., Public Voice, 1986), iii.

[15]Ronald D. Eller, "Poverty Amidst Plenty," *Light*, September 1986, 3-4.

[16]Richard J. Margolis, "How Hunger Staged a Comeback," *Foundation News* 26 (November/December 1985): 22.

[17]*Hunger in America,* 104.

5
The best-kept secret

The best-kept secret in Southern Baptist life is what Southern Baptists are doing at home and abroad about hunger. No one deliberately hides the good news. Indeed many share the message about hunger ministries on a daily basis. Nevertheless, a vast number have yet to hear and then to respond. As more and more Southern Baptists learn the secret, a greater and greater surge of activity will shoot around the globe, making a world of difference in a hungry world.

Of course the entire story cannot be told in just one chapter. But bits and pieces of the story illustrate what Southern Baptists are doing through local churches, associations, state conventions; and the Foreign Mission Board, Home Mission Board, and Brotherhood Commission, all of which are Southern Baptist Convention agencies; and Woman's Missionary Union, Auxiliary to SBC. From sermons to soup kitchens, from drilling wells to distributing educational literature, from writing letters to Congress to writing checks for hunger contributions, Southern Baptist involvement is characterized by diversity.

Foreign Mission Board

When most Southern Baptists think about what the Foreign Mission Board (FMB) does in the area of hunger ministries, we visualize emergency relief. We think about large cargo planes dropping specially wrapped 100-pound sacks of dry grain to mountain people on the brink of starvation or about emaciated children receiving fluids intravenously at a makeshift medical center. What we often overlook is another dimension of hunger ministry called transformation or development work.

Development work is a hand up to self-reliance, helping the hungry help themselves. Contrary to popular opinion, almost two-thirds of hunger funds are now spent on development ministries, compared to 1977 when the FMB allocated almost all its hunger receipts for emergency relief. To appreciate the full scope of the FMB's hunger ministry, we must understand both approaches.

The Foreign Mission Board does a great deal of emergency hunger relief. At the height of the 1983-85 African famine, a Southern Baptist feeding center was set up in the remote highland town of Rabel, Ethiopia. Within the first three weeks of its opening, 7,000 starving people staggered into the camp. Many expressed their deep gratitude by falling to their knees and trying to kiss the feet of missionaries.

Work expanded rapidly in Ethiopia. Soon four other feeding centers were established which fed an estimated 150,000 people each month. One of the special efforts was to feed severely malnourished children who received each day up to six meals—meals which were a porridge mixture composed of wheat, powdered milk, soybean, and sorghum.

Across the continent in Mali, Southern Baptists were also distributing food. Norman and Beverly Coad moved 5,000 tons of grain over 1,000 miles from the coast of West Africa inland to Mali where they distributed it. When the operation ended, the Coads discovered that they had lost less than one tenth of one percent of the grain. Relief officials were surprised, since the standard expected loss was 30 percent.

In addition to Africa, emergency hunger relief efforts are implemented around the world. Floods, typhoons, diseases, and fires often place people at risk to hunger, and in need of emergency hunger relief. And when disasters strike, foreign missionaries respond.

Emergency hunger relief is essential when disasters hit. Displaced people are people with desperate human needs. Equally as important and heroic but without the dramatic appeal is development work—work which helps hungry people help themselves.

Drilling wells may seem mundane. Yet it is pure water that goes a long way toward improving the health of poor people, keeping them from polluted water which is the source of guinea worm, hepatitis, and other diseases. Similarly, building ponds for fishing and irrigation offers help toward self-reliance. Self-reliance is the key to breaking the back of widespread, chronic poverty and malnutrition.

One of the foremost examples of Southern Baptist development efforts is found in the work of Harold Watson, missionary to the Philippines. Watson has introduced a hillside farming technique called Sloping Agricultural Land Technology (SALT) to combat soil erosion and to increase food production.

Thick hedgerows of ipil-ipil trees are planted yards apart down a hillside. Erosion causes the space between the hedgerows to fill in and flatten out, forming a terrace where crops can be grown. The high nitrogen from the foliage of the hedgerows fertilizes the land. Corn, beans, pineapple, coffee, bananas, and sweet potatoes have flourished with such a method of farming.

Each year Filipino farmers and extension workers, US Peace Corps volunteers, and foreign aid officials from Great Britain and the Netherlands travel to Watson's training center. More than 6,000 people visit the center every year! They learn how SALT works and how to transplant it elsewhere.

In 1985 Watson's years of antihunger work were recognized and applauded on an international scale. He received the Asian version of the Nobel Prize, the Ramon Magsaysay Award, becoming one of the few non-Asians ever to win the award in its 28-year history. The award foundation's trustees saluted Watson for working among "the poorest of small farmers."

Numerous other Southern Baptist development projects provide poor people with the technology or resources to move toward self-reliance. In Bangladesh beggars from the worst ghettos learn carpentry and electrical work from missionaries. These simple skills enable them to earn a living rather than to live through begging. In Rwanda over 3,400 people have been trained to build hutches and to raise rabbits with the hope that the rabbit meat will improve the nutritional level of the Rwandans. Each person who passes the training course receives a male and two female rabbits with which to start.

A final clarifying note is necessary. The FMB is not a registered relief agency such as Catholic Relief Services, Lutheran World Relief, CARE, and World Vision. Instead the FMB does hunger work in the context of its overall missions endeavor. Bread for the body and the soul are shared as one, pointing towards God's love for the total human being.

The FMB uses two different categories to assign contributions for its relief ministries. The first is hunger relief; the second is general relief. Both are important human needs ministries, but each has a unique function.

Hunger relief funds are spent on projects such as agriculture, community development, community health, educational assistance, food distribution, nutritional rehabilitation, vocational training, and water. Honduras provides a good example of the use of hunger relief funds in 1986. With $20,000 a vocational training program was started. Men and women received training in mechanics, welding, carpentry, and sewing. Another $15,000 went to provide emergency relief for 50 days to 200 families until the harvest of crops. Over $9,000 was allocated for agricultural self-help programs related to nutrition. And $16,000 went to water drilling to make pure drinking water available for eight communities.

General relief is the second category. These funds are used in areas which do not fit into the category of hunger relief. However, if hunger relief funds run low, general relief funds may be spent for hunger-related needs.

In 1986, general relief funds were spent in a variety of programs. Forty homes destroyed by fire in Pasay City in the Philippines were reconstructed. An eyeglass project was also continued in the Philippines and a church was rebuilt in Malawi.

For more information, write to the Foreign Mission Board, P.O. Box 6767, Richmond, VA 23230.

Home Mission Board

Like the Foreign Mission Board, the Home Mission Board (HMB) conducts hunger ministries. Its scale of operation is smaller, but its commitment to stretching hunger receipts as far as possible is similar. One-hundred percent of domestic hunger funds are spent on food assistance. Through local churches and Baptist associations, the HMB distributes hunger gifts in almost every state.

Domestic hunger funds meet hunger needs in a variety of ways. The Missouri Baptist Convention in 1985 received $50,000 for the distribution of food to families suffering from the farm crisis. These funds were channeled through the Missouri Baptist Convention Missions Department to associational directors of missions and, in turn, to local churches. But the pride of farm families made the distribution of funds difficult. A direct approach seldom worked. Churches found that one way to help was through second parties—families using hunger funds to help neighboring families.

In recent years, domestic hunger funds started seven new food closets in the Birmingham Baptist Association in Alabama; enabled the Palm Lake Baptist Association to distribute food packets designed to meet the needs of a family for three days; and provided food assistance to 500 families in McComb, Mississippi. Almost 27,000 meals were served to transients and the homeless at the Brantley Baptist Center, New Orleans, Louisiana. The three Baptist centers in Houston, Texas, were also fighting hunger. In addition to using $10,000 in domestic hunger funds in 1987, they distributed 500,000 loaves of bread, 300,000 dozen doughnuts, and 325,000 pounds of rice, all of which are donated to the centers.

Besides requesting hunger funds from the HMB, many home missionaries tap into local resources. Jack Little, director of church and community ministries and church extension for the Chattahoochee Baptist Association, Georgia, has used the area chicken industry. He has persuaded a chicken farm in Gainesville, Georgia, to donate 720 eggs to the association's food pantry each month.

Another home missionary, Nathan Porter, national consultant for disaster relief, domestic hunger and migrant ministries, conducts hunger surveys, enabling churches to pinpoint the hungry in their own communities. His surveys locate the needy, identify local resources, and find the gaps which Baptists can fill. (The Local Hunger Survey Guide is available free from Orders Processing, Home Mission Board, 1350 Spring Street N.W., Atlanta, GA 30367-5601.)

Where does your money go?

The Southern Baptist hunger ministry is unique in that 100 percent of hunger gifts go to meet hunger needs, compared to many hunger organizations that spend 25 percent or more on fund raising and administration. The Foreign Mission Board sends money overseas as designated. It is not spent stateside for promotion or administration. Similarly, the Home Mission Board distributes 100 percent of all hunger gifts on the purchase of food. The Cooperative Program and the Lottie Moon Christmas Offering for Foreign Missions and Annie Armstrong Easter Offering for Home Missions offerings support the work of missionaries, providing the support structure which allows the entire hunger dollar to go to meet hunger needs.

Undesignated hunger contributions sent to SBC agencies are divided with 80 percent going to the Foreign Mission Board and 20 percent going to the Home Mission Board, in accordance with the division suggestions approved by SBC messengers in 1981. Several Baptist state conventions, however, still send almost all their hunger receipts to the FMB. Others spend a considerable percentage of the hunger contributions on the local level or for special foreign missions projects related to hunger.

Woman's Missionary Union and Brotherhood Commission

Across the nation, Baptist women, girls, men, and boys engage in missions projects related to hunger. They study the issue and do much of the work. They are the bedrock of the Southern Baptist effort to care for an impoverished world.

Examples of what Baptist Women organizations and Girls in Action are doing are numerous. At Rich Road Baptist Church, Raleigh, North Carolina, Baptist Women bring bags of food each month for the Shepherd's Table soup kitchen. Others staff the center as volunteers. At the Baptist Indian Center, Salt Lake City, Utah, Baptist Women make lunches available Monday through Friday for impoverished school children. As for involvement of Girls in Action, at the Eastern Hills Baptist Church, Montgomery, Alabama, girls gave up a soft drink per week and gave the money to buy ducklings for a hunger project in Bangladesh.

From hunger races to raising potatoes, Baptist men and boys also engage in mission support and mission action projects. At the 1986 National Pioneer Hunger Race in Memphis, Tennessee, over 300 Royal Ambassadors and their counselors raced more than two miles, raising over $7,500 for world hunger. Another group raised potatoes, not money, for the needy. The men of Ararat Baptist Church, Jackson, Tennessee, planted six acres and produced 100,000 pounds of Irish potatoes for the four Baptist children's homes of Tennessee. Mission action is an integral part of both WMU and Brotherhood.

Baptist state conventions

Baptist state conventions address the hunger issue in diverse ways. Almost all do some direct hunger ministries. Many engage in raising the level of awareness and providing educational information. A few participate directly in hunger projects abroad in partnership with the FMB. Three Baptist state conventions illustrate what many state conventions are doing or could do to feed the hungry and to help the hungry feed themselves.

The Louisiana Baptist Convention offers one model for involvement. It has an active world hunger committee composed of 13 members from across the state. Founded in 1980, this committee produces a quarterly newsletter, promotes the observance of World Hunger Day on the SBC calendar, and sponsors hunger awareness events. The fact that Louisiana Baptist hunger gifts have soared from $5,799 in 1977 to an all time high of $302,559 in 1985 indicates the committee's influence.

A second model is that of the Kentucky Baptist Convention. For a number of years Kentucky Baptists have responded to human needs. However, the convention has launched a program to sponsor four regional human needs conferences each year for five years. The purpose is to raise the level of awareness, to equip churches for ministry, to gather information, and to prepare a module for use in local churches for years to come. Over 500 Kentuckians have participated since the program began in 1986.

A third model is the Baptist State Convention of North Carolina's three and-half year missions partnership with Togo. North Carolina's venture has addressed many of the hunger-related difficulties facing the people near the village of Moretan: over 100 wells were drilled with pumps installed: 16 ponds were built; a 200-foot concrete bridge was constructed; and a pharmacy was built. Such development work ensures that water is available even in dry season, that fresh water diminishes the problems arising from the use of unsanitary water, and that health care is accessible.

Baptist associations

Baptist associations are the cornerstone to meeting hunger needs on a cooperative basis at the local level. Three associations serve as examples of the diversity of approaches: Blue River-Kansas City Baptist Association in Missouri, Tarrant Baptist Association in Texas, and Long Run Baptist Association in Kentucky.

For the past several years, the Blue River-Kansas City Baptist Association has sponsored hunger rallies, followed by hunger walks which have raised over $30,000. The rally motivates and informs participants, while the walk is a fund-raising event. Both undergird the direct hunger ministries of the association.

The money contributed at the hunger walks plus domestic hunger funds from the HMB have assisted the association to serve food to 9,422 families or 28,298 people in 1986, a 40 percent increase from 1985. The association, however, has not been satisfied with only these sources of support. It has also taken advantage of fresh produce donated by supermarkets and government commodities, all of which have been distributed through its ten service centers. Churches and church members have also been enlisted. A rural church has grown gardens for the hungry. Some church members have prepared meals for the homeless at the shelter housed in the Forest Avenue Baptist Church, and other church members have conducted nutrition classes.

Another example is the Tarrant Baptist Association in Fort Worth, Texas, which has used hunger funds from the HMB for three years. Through its community center and an effort called Urban Allies, the association operates a food voucher program. Needy people receive a voucher at the community center or from an associational worker making a home visit. With the voucher, the recipient purchases food at a local grocery store. The grocery store, in turn, submits the voucher to the associational office for reimbursement. The program ensures that hunger funds go for hunger needs.

The Long Run Baptist Association in Louisville, Kentucky, has operated for four years an effort called the Infant Resource Project. With hunger funds from the HMB, low-income mothers with newborns are provided formula and food. Since hunger funds may only be spent for food, the association supplies beds, diapers, bottles, and other necessities from other sources. An estimated 260 families have obtained assistance in 1987.

Baptist churches

A large number of Baptist churches have some form of hunger ministry. In fact, the evidence is startling. Over 130 of the 162 churches and missions in the Nashville Baptist Association, Nashville, Tennessee, participate each year in a peanut butter food drive for Second Harvest Food Bank. The Union Baptist Association, Houston, Texas, reports that 152 of its 240 churches have programs which meet food needs, while the missions department of the Missouri Baptist Convention estimates three-fourths of its churches either stock food pantries or participate in community food banks.

Among the most unusual examples of what Southern Baptist

churches are doing about hunger are First Baptist Church, Spartanburg, South Carolina, and Parkwood Baptist Church, Annandale, Virginia. Each has a unique focus.

At First Baptist Spartanburg, Rice Bowl, Inc. is a hunger ministry with a worldwide impact. When the church's pastor, Alastair Walker, was elected president of the South Carolina Baptist Convention in 1979, he said he wanted to place a plastic rice bowl on the table of every church member in the convention by the end of the year. The purpose was to remind church members about the world's food crisis and to collect money.

Nine years later, close to 1 million rice bowls have been distributed, and tens of millions of dollars have been raised. Bowls have been distributed across the SBC. Over 15,000 have been sent to the Republic of South Africa. Each bowl costs 40 cents, but has the capacity to hold about $12. (For more information, write: Rice Bowl, Inc., P. 0. Box 3216, Spartanburg, SC 29304.)

Through its hunger committee, the Parkwood Baptist Church, Annandale, Virginia, has established an impressive record of a holistic ministry. World hunger giving has increased from $731 in 1979 to a high of $11,811 in 1985. Accompanying the rise in hunger giving has been a steady increase in giving to the Lottie Moon Christmas Offering.

Started in 1981, the hunger committee has distributed rice bowls, sponsored a feeding program in Haiti, supported an emergency grain shipment to Ghana, and maintained a food closet. It has also taken a step beyond the collection of money and direct ministry by becoming involved in public policy. Its members have engaged in antihunger legislation through letter-writing campaigns, as well as through membership in Bread for the World, a Christian citizens' lobby on food and hunger issues.

The Missions Development Council in the church can initiate and coordinate hunger projects for that church.

Baptist educational institutions

Two Southern Baptist educational institutions highlight activism on the hunger issue: Southern Baptist Theological Seminary in Louisville, Kentucky, and Carson Newman College in Jefferson City, Tennessee. Both illustrate what others are doing and offer models for what can be done on school campuses.

Founded in the spring of 1976 at Southern Baptist Theological Seminary, Seminarians United Against Hunger (SUAH) addresses the issue on multiple levels. For ten years, SUAH has raised the level of awareness among and educated seminarians who minister around the world. It has regularly sent donations to a FMB fish farm and village development project in Bangladesh. Additionally, SUAH members serve in soup kitchens, participate in citywide hunger walks, collect canned goods for food drives, and engage in miss-a-meal devotional programs.

One core activity has been the practice of Christian citizenship. Besides encouraging seminarians to join Bread for the World, SUAH coordinates letter-writing campaigns to Congress on hunger issues each year. (Over 400 students in 1987 wrote their US congressmen urging them to support legislation to increase funding for a special supplemental feeding program for women, infants, and children.) SUAH members recognized that compassion and citizenship go hand in hand.

Another active hunger group is the Baptist Student Union at Carson Newman College. Through a BSU ministry called Appalachian Outreach, students form a partnership with people in poverty, helping to restore the self-esteem of and to provide necessities of life to the impoverished. Students support a shelter for the homeless, work at a food pantry, repair homes, teach home management (nutrition, personal hygiene, cooking, sewing, and budgeting), and provide assistance with literacy training.

The best-kept secret in Southern Baptist life is what Southern Baptists are doing at home and abroad about hunger. It is a secret which ought to be told widely. Good news is only good news when shared. Tell the secret to others, so they too may become involved.

The next time someone asks, What can we do about hunger? point out what others are doing. If your church, association, state convention, or educational institution is only marginally active on the hunger issue, consider adapting one of the models profiled in this chapter. The diversity of responses ensures that every entity can find some way to be involved. Moreover, the sterling work of the mission boards offers Southern Baptists an opportunity to feed the hungry and to help the hungry feed themselves across the nation and around the world.

6
What shall we do?

What shall we do? is one of the most disturbing questions facing Christians as they hold a newspaper in one hand and the Bible in the other. We have a morning devotional, and then on the way to work in wintry weather we see a crippled street woman pushing a shopping cart loaded with all her treasures. Or we listen to a Sunday morning sermon on love for neighbor only to turn on the television after lunch to see a barefoot Latin American child dressed in rags playing in a filthy sewer ditch. We immediately ask ourselves, What shall we do?

We are not the first people to face such a question, however. Down through the ages it has troubled Christians, refusing to let them alone and forcing them to decide between responsible action and irresponsible inaction. The dilemma bothered even the people of the New Testament world.

"What then shall we do?" pleaded the multitudes to John the Baptist when he called for the bearing of "fruits that befit repentance" (Luke 3:7-14). A rich ruler raised a similar question: "What shall I do to inherit eternal life?" (Luke 18:18-23).

Each answer called for concrete action. John the Baptist said in part: "He who has two coats, let him share with him who has none; and he who has food, let him do likewise" (Luke 3:11). As for the rich ruler, Jesus told him: "Sell all that you have and distribute to the poor, and you will have treasure in heaven; and come, follow me" (Luke 18:22).

This chapter suggests *what* we can do to respond to worldwide hunger, as well as *how* we can do it. The action suggestions may not appeal to everyone. People are different. Some may feel called to mission action projects; others may be drawn to political activism. We are not all called to do the same thing, but we are all called to do something.

We may each decide to take different concrete steps. Nevertheless, we may all benefit from a word of wisdom about social change: "think globally; act locally." We need to keep the big picture in mind, while we act where we live. The linchpin in the strategy against hunger is a world view and local initiative.

Evangelism

Social change begins with a change of heart. No two biblical accounts make this point more clearly than the conversion of Zacchaeus and the rejection of the rich ruler. Both are models of the relationship between conversion and social change.

When Zacchaeus heard the good news from and experienced the love of Jesus, he turned abruptly from his old ways. He moved in a new direction, leaving behind a life-style of economic injustice to pursue economic justice for all. His change of heart resulted in a change for the impoverished who lived around him. Such was not the case of the rich ruler who rejected Jesus' call to new life. He hung on to his old life-style. And the impoverished around him remained impoverished.

Christian conversion is the beginning point for social involvement. It should give birth to a new way of thinking about and seeing God's created order and the Christian's role in it. Conversion should entail freeing the believer from the commitment of secular ideology to the challenge of God's kingdom.

But oftentimes Christian conversion does not transform the way we relate to the world. Stephen Charles Mott, professor of Christian social ethics at Gordon-Conwell Theological Seminary, notes: "Bible Belt conversions resulted in no general change with respect to racial segregation, nor did northern fundamentalist conversions result in more just relationships between the classes of the industrial structure."[1]

A change of heart should be synonymous with a change in attitude. And American Christians need desperately to transform the way we think about the poor. Because we see them as the world does, we fail to see the genuine hardness of their plight and we fail to love. Only with a renewal of mind can we begin to approach "what is good and acceptable and perfect" (Rom. 12:2).

Any long-term response to worldwide hunger begins with a transformation of our hearts and minds.

Education

Knowledge is a powerful resource in the war on hunger. The more we know, the more we can understand the causes of hunger, as well as devise and advocate realistic strategies against hunger.

Awareness/Action

Global hunger awareness and action should permeate the entire church. Sunday School classes, Church Training programs, mission action committees, and other local church committees should focus intently on the issue. Additionally, a local church needs to engage in citizenship action related to hunger issues. Awareness raising and action implementing have a twofold purpose: one internal and the other external.

The first leavens the entire church, raising the level of awareness, providing educational programs, and calling for social action.

The other function is to provide leadership in the local community. The church through appropriate leadership and organization can speak to hunger issues in public meetings and on current legislation. The pastor need not be the only spokesperson, however. Lay involvement broadens the base from which a church speaks to moral issues.

When a church addresses hunger issues in public, diverse representation is a prerequisite for effectiveness. Diversity of political affiliation, professional occupation, and economic classification is critical. City councils and legislative committees are more likely to hear the concerns of a church if the group speaking reflects a broad base.

Mapping hunger

One way to learn about hunger through experience is to map it. Finding out where the poor live, what public or private assistance is available, and how needy people reach town or travel across town expands awareness. Here are suggestions for how to map hunger in your community:

1. After getting a map of your community, divide the group into different task forces. Assign one to find the low-income neighborhoods, the largest-area employers, and the public transportation routes between the two. Ask another to locate area shelters,

soup kitchens, and food pantries. Once these facilities are found, determine what services are offered. Request a third group to identify the various public assistance offices such as the food stamp office and job training programs. Also give them the task of pinpointing the homes where the federally sponsored program called Meals on Wheels is served.

2. Use different colored pins to mark the map with the gathered data. Then discuss as a group the difficulties poor people face: How do they travel from home to work? Are the food pantries located near poverty neighborhoods? Is the food stamp office accessible for the rural poor? Where does a homeless family go for shelter? Do job training programs provide care for single mothers with young children? Where are the soup kitchens that serve breakfast? Which food pantries are open seven days a week?

The exercise of mapping hunger educates church people to real-life problems. It can identify weak spots and strong points in the antihunger network. It can also break down stereotypes which cripple understanding.

Mission action

At the heart of the Christian message resides the mandate to meet human needs, which many seek to fulfill through mission action projects. Laypersons do missions when they volunteer to work in soup kitchens or rescue missions. They do missions as short-term medical personnel, irrigation specialists, nutritionists, agriculturalists, and veterinarians. Two examples of mission action projects for churches or church groups are gleaning and food drives.

Gleaning

Gleaning the unharvested produce from farm fields offers one mission action project which turns the problem of wasted food into a solution to hunger. If just a fraction of the 60 million tons of food which rots in American fields were harvested, it would go a long way to meeting temporary food needs. Keep the following general points in mind when considering gleaning:

1. Check to see if your state has a Good Samaritan law which would protect the farmer and the missions volunteer from liability in case of accidental injury or property damage. If no law exists, either obtain insurance or have waivers signed. Of course, working

through the state legislature to enact such a law would be a valuable contribution.

2. Find a local farmer willing to participate and an organization such as a local food bank or rescue mission willing to accept the products gleaned. Work out all the arrangements with the donor and the recipient agency.

3. Train the volunteers. Urge them to respect the farm property and expect a lot of work. Remember to instruct them about what to wear (such as gloves and sturdy old shoes), to supply them with tools (such as knives, ladders, and containers), and to provide them with plenty of water and snacks. Be sure to have a first-aid kit.

4. Secure a place to clean the produce. Weigh the food for your records. Also, consider storing and packing the food.

5. Deliver the produce to the distribution or feeding center.

For more information, contact the following organizations: Harvest of Hope, 14512 Beach Road, Chesterfield, VA 23832, (804) 229-5956; and Second Harvest National Food Bank Network, The Fisher Building, 343 South Dearborn, Suite 410, Chicago, IL 60604, (312) 341-1303.

Food drive

Community food pantries face a daily battle to keep their shelves stocked for the constant stream of needy people. The demand for food does not drop off when the food supply does. People need canned goods, baby formula, and bread every day.

Sponsoring a food drive is one mission action project that has the immediate impact of replenishing empty shelves at food pantries. Like other projects, it can be a rewarding effort pursued successfully at a number of levels. A local church can have a food drive for a specific item, such as peanut butter. Or an association of churches can sponsor an event for a nutritionally balanced bag of groceries.

Another type of food drive targets grocery stores. The idea is not to get the store to donate food, although that too is a good idea. Rather, customers can drop a food item or two into a box as they leave the store. Here are some guidelines:

1. Gather as much information as possible from the area food pantry about what its food needs are, how many people request assistance, and who sponsors the pantry. This information helps the grocery store manager make his or her decision about par-

ticipation. It also enables volunteers to respond accurately to questions which shoppers may ask. Consider distributing a fact sheet about area poverty and food needs to consumers.

2. Obtain permission from the grocery store to conduct a food drive on a specific date and time. Assure the manager shoppers will not be disturbed and litter from the drive will be cleaned up.

3. Prepare volunteers for service. Encourage participants to learn the facts about the area food needs and the food pantry. Make sure one or more people will staff the food drive table and food box the entire time of the event.

4. Publicize the date and time with public service announcements on local radio and news releases in community newspapers. Include information about who is sponsoring the food drive and to whom the food will be distributed.

5. Affirm the people who make donations and thank the grocery store with a personal letter. Share the success of the project with the editor of your state Baptist newspaper, requesting a news story.

Mission action projects remain a primary way for Christians to meet hunger needs. The suggestions of gleaning and food drives represent only two of many possible projects.

Stewardship

When most church members consider the issue of stewardship, they usually think first of the church budget, tithing, and special missions offerings. Of course, Christian stewardship encompasses more than strict concern about money. The larger picture emphasizes all creation, all possessions, and all gifts. Stewardship is really an issue of life-style.

We should remember that the entire created order belongs to God. It is God's handiwork, God's garden. Human beings have been made caretakers of creation (Gen. 1:28-30) with the expectation that we will use it for the common good (Isa. 58:7-8). Comprehensive stewardship applies to every area of life, including how we use professional skills, give money, and invest money.

Professional skills

Stewardship is more than giving money to Christian causes. We practice stewardship with professional gifts, skills, training, and time. For individuals, stewardship may mean volunteering medical skills in an inner-city clinic one day a month, serving as a nutritionist for a soup kitchen, helping a food bank with its bookkeeping, or offering free legal advice to poor families. For other church groups, stewardship may mean repairing the homes of the poor or preparing meals for a storefront mission.

Giving

A number of proposals have challenged Southern Baptists to increase hunger giving. A minimum of $1.00 per person has been a popular suggestion. Missing one meal each week and donating the money to hunger ministries has been another. The most daring challenge comes from a 1987 Missouri Baptist Convention resolution which urges church members to give a dime a day. If this goal were achieved, each church member would give $36.50 annually, and the state convention would give $22,848,562 annually, much more than its all-time high of $442,352.

Ronald Sider, professor of theology at Eastern Baptist Theological Seminary, has made one of the most radically sounding and yet practical suggestions concerning stewardship. It is called a graduated tithe. Here is how it works:

1. A family decides to tithe 10 percent of their earnings to the church.

2. They determine how much is needed to live on, including future expenses such as college for their children.

3. They covenant that 5 percent above the basic tithe for every $1,000 increase in income will be given away. Such a strategy makes far more money available for kingdom work![2]

Investments

Besides giving money, stewardship involves how we invest money. As individuals, we invest money in retirement plans, mutual funds, and the stock market. We save money in banks and through other financial institutions. Churches, Christian schools, state conventions, and denominational agencies also invest huge sums of money.

With the total wealth of churches in the US well in excess of $160 billion, investments could be used to accomplish moral objectives. They could be an untapped resource to use against poverty. Rather than believe that investments are morally neutral, we must recognize that they may cause good or harm. We need to encourage Christian institutions to avoid investments in corporations which perpetuate poverty, injustice, environmental destruction, and war. Christian institutions ought to seek a sound return on investments, while making a witness to Christ in a secular marketplace.

Citizenship

An excellent illustration of the relationship between charity and citizenship occurred in 1985. The Live Aid global rock concert raised pledges of $70 million that summer for the hungry in Africa. It was a highly visible, much talked about event. Meanwhile, an almost unnoticed lobbying effort on the part of Christians, led by Bread for the World, pushed through Congress an $800 million food assistance program for Africa. Both were important events. The latter had a far greater impact. The lesson from these two events was clear: public legislation is far too important to ignore!

The authors of *Endangered Species* present a similar case, not from pragmatic but theological grounds:

> The neglect of personal political responsibility surrenders to ignorance and indifference. It encourages political powers to draw the wrong conclusions and to make the wrong decisions. To fail to make feelings known about critical decisions is worse than bad citizenship. It is sin. It is simply a more sophisticated way of walking on the other side of the road, ignoring the one who suffers. It is a clear evidence, a testimony, of unconcern.[3]

True concern manifests itself in a practice which refuses to divorce Christian faith and public policy.[4]

Political involvement is an essential extension of Christian faith. Faith, however, does not shield Christians in politics from failure or bad decisions. Christians can make mistakes just like non-Christians. Thus, it is doubly important for Christians in politics to recall Jesus' words to "be wise as serpents."

Christians manifest wisdom when they harbor no illusions about politics. "Meaningful Christian involvement requires not only ideals and visions, but also a willingness to get dirt under one's fingernails out in the real political world. And the real political world is indeed a tough, risky, sweaty place."[5]

With a firm handhold on the extent of Christian faith and the nature of politics, we next ask how to practice Christian citizenship.

Letter writing

Letter writing to elected officials is one way to practice Christian citizenship. State and national representatives cannot read the public mind. They can read their mail, however. Just a few letters have been known to determine how an elected official votes. Sen.

Paul Simon (D-Ill.) has said, "Someone who sits down and writes a letter about hunger . . . almost literally has to be saving a life."[6] Here are simple steps to remember about letter writing:

1. Keep your letter brief. Write only a few sentences focusing on a specific issue.

2. Keep your letter in your own words. Form letters can be spotted a mile off. They carry less weight than an individual letter.

3. Keep your letter respectful. Arrogance, meanness, bullying, and rudeness turn off staff aides. The people who read the letters are human beings. Treat them kindly. Disagreement can be expressed courteously.

4. Keep your letter timely. Contact your legislator when a matter is under consideration or before a final vote is taken.

In addition to letters, express your opinion with telephone calls. The guidelines that apply to letters also apply to telephone calls. When making a call, remember in what time zone the nation's capital is located and recognize that you will speak with a congressional aide. Mailgrams and telegrams are others ways to communicate rapidly with governmental officials.

The following are some key addresses and phone numbers:

The Honorable (Name)
US Senate
Washington, DC 20001
(202) 224-3121

The Honorable (Name)
US House of Representatives
Washington, DC 20001
(202) 224-3121

The President
The White House
Washington, DC 20500
(202) 456-1414

Public forums

Elected officials constantly attend public meetings, seeking to build support for their next election. They hold meetings in public libraries, schools, civic centers, and even at shopping malls. In order to attract a crowd, they announce these meetings in advance. Regrettably, only a small percentage of the voting public ever attends.

Attending public forums offers another way to practice citizenship. Kim Bobo, author of *Lives Matter: A Handbook for Christian Organizing*, contends that raising questions is a form of lobbying: "Elected leaders judge community concerns by the kinds of questions that are asked."[7] And Christians cannot ask questions without going to town hall meetings.

Sen. Jim Sasser (D-Tenn.) held a series of meetings across Tennessee in 1985. At one of the earliest meetings, he was asked about his support for the International Agency for Agricultural Development (IFAD). He expressed no knowledge of this agency. The question was asked at the second stop. And again, he said he was unfamiliar with it. When the question was raised at the third public forum, he determined to find out about IFAD. Senator Sasser became a cosponsor of legislation about which his constituency had expressed interest.

Of course all public forums do not translate into success stories. Failure and compromise characterize politics. Yet, attending public forums is one way to practice citizenship.

Inviting public officials to speak

Invite elected leaders to a church forum. It is easy to organize, since church members are already committed to attending a regularly scheduled church service. Furthermore, it offers a backdrop which most elected officials find attractive.

Remember these general ideas for a special evening at church with an elected leader:

1. Invite the person several months in advance to speak at a churchwide hunger banquet.

2. Help the elected leader to decide what topic to address with several suggestions such as the nature of US food aid, the status of current reforms in the welfare program, what the US ought to do to end hunger in Latin America, and what antihunger initiatives deserve special public support.

3. Build in time for the participants to ask questions concerning the topic addressed.

4. Know the elected official's record well enough to affirm publicly his or her leadership. Do not praise a weak record. Do affirm the positive aspects of a voting record.

Inviting elected leaders to speak at a church meeting accomplishes something besides letting them know that Christians care about how public policy affects the hungry. It forces them and their aides to study the hunger issue. The more they learn, the better the possibility that they will support responsible legislation.

[1]Stephen Charles Mott, *Biblical Ethics and Social Change* (New York: Oxford Press, 1982), 114.

[2]Ronald J. Sider, *Rich Christians in an Age of Hunger: A Biblical Study*, Revised and Expanded (Downers Grove, Ill.: Inter-Varsity Press, 1984), 166-69.

[3]James M. Dunn, Ben E. Loring, and Phil D. Strickland, *Endangered Species* (Nashville: Broadman Press, 1976), 105.

[4]Arthur Simon, *Christian Faith and Public Policy: No Grounds for Divorce* (Grand Rapids: William B. Eerdmans Publishing Company, 1987).

[5]Stephen V. Monsma, *Pursuing Justice in a Sinful World* (Grand Rapids: William B. Eerdmans Publishing Company, 1984), 3.

[6]*1985-1986 World Hunger Awareness/Action Guide* (Nashville: Christian Life Commission), 16.

[7]Kimberly Bobo, *Lives Matter: A Handbook for Christian Organizing* (Kansas City: Sheed and Ward, 1986), 231. This is an excellent book which concentrates on how to work against hunger.

7
On the front line: Three special Christian organizations

World hunger day is every day. An estimated 730 million people around the world face each day with little prospects of having enough food.[1] They are chronically malnourished, despite the fact that the "world today produces enough grain alone to provide every human being on the planet with 3,600 calories a day."[2]

From the very beginning hunger has been a human problem. The struggle for food is captured in the words from God to Adam: "Cursed is the ground because of you; in toil you shall eat of it all the days of your life; thorns and thistles it shall bring forth to you; and you shall eat the plants of the field. In the sweat of your face you shall eat bread till you return to the ground" (Gen. 3:17-19).

Against the rock-hard reality of hunger has been the vision of bountiful food: "May there be abundance of grain in the land; on the tops of the mountains may it wave; may its fruit be like Lebanon" (Psalm 72:16). The vision reappears in Micah's hope of universal peace when weapons of war are converted into tools of agriculture and people own productive fields (Micah 4:1-4).

The vision of a world without hunger is often shattered against the sun baked soil of human failure. Lofty dreams often never touch the ground of human suffering. Over and over again, churches have passed resolutions, politicians have made pronouncements, and international agencies have made declarations about ending hunger. Yet hunger is not vanquished.

At the United Nations-sponsored World Food Conference in 1974, delegates accepted a challenge from US Secretary of State Henry

Kissinger. They proclaimed "that within a decade no child will go to bed hungry, that no family will fear for its next day's bread and that no human being's future and capacities will be stunted by malnutrition."[3] Almost exactly a decade later, the news accounts about the mass starvation in Ethiopia shocked the world. The soaring rhetoric of the past had done little to prevent suffering. The global community did not have the determination to pursue its vision.

The failure to end hunger does not mean that governments and nongovernmental organizations have been inactive. Many have made important strides in increasing the availability of food. Without their actions, the world could be even hungrier.

Among some of the most active organizations are church-related groups. Literally hundreds of Christian organizations battle hunger through emergency relief, agricultural development, education, and public policy.

In the frontlines stand three unique Christian organizations: Bread for the World, Habitat for Humanity, and *Seeds*. Each complements the efforts of Christian denominations and offers avenues for increased involvement.

Bread for the World

What is the purpose of Bread for the World?

When seven Protestants and seven Catholics met in October 1973 in New York City, they recognized two facts about churches in a hungry world. First, churches were waist-deep in direct-feeding ministries. Second, Christians could get at the root causes of hunger through governmental policies, if they were organized to influence Congress and the White House. Not wanting to duplicate relief and development ministries, the group determined to start a grass-roots Christian citizen's movement to influence US government policies to end hunger.

At the birth of Bread for the World was a man named Art Simon whose parents had been Lutheran missionaries to China. His family background plus his education at Concordia Seminary and experience in the pastorate of a small inner-city church in the New York City's Lower East Side prepared him for the leadership of Bread for the World.

Fourteen years after the first meeting, Simon is still at the helm, keeping Bread on its original course. Today it remains the only Christian citizens' lobby in the nation's capital which works solely on hunger issues.

Who belongs to Bread for the World?

Membership is open to the public, with no particular doctrinal stance required. All that is necessary is a $25 membership fee or $15 for students. Churches may join through the Covenant Church Program which entails a $250 membership fee.

Bread has grown from 400 paying members in 1974 to more than 40,500 in 1987. Almost 5 percent of its members identify themselves as Baptists, compared to 37 percent Catholic, 13 percent Presbyterian, and 11 percent Lutheran. Four of the 40-member board of directors are Southern Baptists, two of whom served concurrent terms as presidents (James M. Dunn, 1985, and Patricia Ayres, 1986-87).

What are the sources of Bread for the World's income and where is it spent?

Bread's 1986 budget was slightly over $2.4 million. About 75 percent of the annual budget comes from membership fees and special contributions. Other funds are derived from grants and the sale of materials. None of its income comes from federal funds.

As for expenses, about $400,000 in 1986 was spent on administration, while $60,000 went for fund raising. Almost $500,000 was allocated for member lobbying and organizing. Each year an audited financial statement is available upon request.

How does Bread for the World work?

A staff of 70, including 19 interns and volunteers, works in four different departments: Information Services, Issues, Organizing, and Outreach. Each department complements the activities of the others. The Issues Department, for example, testifies before congressional committees and develops support materials for Bread members. In turn, the Organizing Department informs and urges members to contact their elected leaders about timely issues. The lodestar of Bread is its membership, in almost all of the 425 congressional districts, which lobbies their respective US congressmen and senators. Members are kept abreast of current legislation through monthly "action alert" bulletins and quarterly magazines with in-depth yet concise articles. Additionally, the national staff calls congressional district coordinators when Congress considers key hunger-related issues. District coordinators, in turn, activate a telephone network, resulting in local members calling their elected leaders. The telephone networks, called

Quicklines, have generated 10,000 calls to the capital on a single issue.

What has Bread for the World accomplished?

From the very beginning, Bread has worked with tireless pragmatism. The result has been an amazing list of legislative accomplishments, ranging from the 1976 Right to Food resolutions in which Congress set forth a statement of principles on hunger to the 1986 reauthorization of the House Select Committee on Hunger. Other successes include reform of the food stamp program in 1977, the establishment of an emergency grain reserve for famine in 1980, and the redirecting of a greater percentage of US foreign aid to the absolutely poor.

For more information, write Bread for the World, 802 Rhode Island Avenue, N.E., Washington, DC 20018.

Habitat for Humanity

What is the purpose of Habitat for Humanity?

A nutshell answer is "no more shacks!" Habitat pursues one vision: the elimination of poverty housing through a partnership between the haves and the have-nots. Its purpose is to ensure that everyone has a decent place to live.

Habitat's story began with the conversion of Millard Fuller and his move to Koinonia Farm. Before age 30, Millard Fuller, an Alabamian, had become a millionaire only to discover that making money was not enough and that his marriage was breaking up. Fuller gave up the former and saved the latter. In 1968, the Fullers joined Koinonia Farm.

That same year, Clarence Jordan, a Southern Baptist founder of Koinonia Farm, set in motion the creation of the Fund for Humanity. He envisioned a partnership in which Christians with financial resources enabled the poor to obtain noninterest-bearing loans for farming, industries, and housing. "What the poor need," Jordan wrote in an open letter to supporters, "is not charity but capital, not caseworkers but co-workers."[4]

Over time the dream grew. The Fund for Humanity evolved into Habitat for Humanity in 1976. Despite the organizational change, Fuller retains the belief that:

> The concept of no profit and no interest is absolutely essential in building homes for the poor. Interest is a burden that keeps poor people locked into their situation. It is a great barrier that they cannot climb over to escape their miserable

life-style. But Jesus' followers don't have to make a profit—they are more interested in people than in profits.[5]

Not only did Jesus' economics influence Fuller, but so did Moses' command found in Exodus 22:25: "If you lend money to any of my people with you who is poor, . . . you shall not exact interest from him."

Who belongs to Habitat for Humanity?

Habitat is an ecumenical Christian movement without a doctrinal statement. Fuller has said:

> We use what we call the theology of the hammer. We may disagree on how to baptize folks; we may disagree on when to take communion. . . . But Christians can agree on the imperative of the gospel, which is to help our neighbors in need. So we can take up hammers and together . . . drive nails and express our common love of Christ as we build houses for God's people in need.[6]

As such, Habitat's board of directors reflects the diversity of Christian denominations.

In 1986, over 100,000 people contributed to Habitat through financial gifts and other forms of support. At its headquarters in Americus, Georgia, 312 volunteers put in 129,000 hours of work, supplementing the work of the 27 paid staff members and 24 support employees.

Beyond individual membership and volunteer work, two other avenues for membership exist. First is affiliation. An affiliate project is a nonprofit, self-supporting, independent organization which has its own board and committee structure. Second is a sponsored project which has its own local board. However, its operational funds come from the international office of Habitat. Most sponsored projects are located in developing nations.

What is the source of Habitat's income and where is it spent?

Habitat's combined income from the affiliated and sponsored projects totaled $13,782,514 in 1986. Gifts ranged in size from $1 to $600,000. Corporate and foundation gifts were $2,063,654, more than ten times the amount in 1985. Individual donations represented a larger percentage of income than those from corporation and foundations.

As for disbursements, over $1.2 million went for fund raising, $715,000 was spent on public awareness and education, and less than $400,000 was allocated for administration. Roughly $9.7 million went into building projects. Each year an audited financial statement is available upon request.

How does Habitat for Humanity work?

"Sweat equity" is a guiding principle. It requires that the future homeowners become partners from the planning stage through the completion of the building. The equity they put down is hard work, typically between 500 to 1,000 hours of construction time. Houses are not built *for* others. Rather, houses are built *with* future homeowners.

The local board determines the nature of the construction, providing the financing and materials. At the completion of a house, it is sold at no profit and financed with a no-interest mortgage. House payments are based upon the ability of the homeowner to pay over a fixed period of time. In turn, the house payments go back into a general pool out of which future funds are drawn to build more houses.

What has Habitat accomplished?

Habitat has built approximately 2,500 houses in ten years. However, construction increases at an accelerated rate with each passing year.

In 1986 the number of affiliate projects dramatically increased from 117 to 171, a 46 percent increase. Habitat constructed or rehabilitated a total of 240 units. As for sponsored projects, 290 houses were built, representing a 36 percent increase, while projects were under way in 18 underdeveloped nations.

For more information, write Habitat for Humanity, Habitat and Church Streets, Americus, GA 31709.

Seeds

What is the purpose of *Seeds?*

Seeds is a nonprofit, education magazine with the goal of encouraging and equipping Christians to respond to hunger within the United States and around the world. It offers in-depth analysis of the political, economic, and environmental causes of hunger, as well as practical how-to articles. Its writers are some of the foremost experts in the field of hunger concerns.

Seeds envisions its journalistic role within the hunger movement as one of undergirding the work of those fighting hunger and interpreting the movement to itself. As such it is both a servant and a constructive critic.

Seeds was started in 1976 by the hunger committee at Oakhurst Baptist Church in Decatur, Georgia. Andy Loving, a recent graduate of Southern Baptist Theological Seminary, and Gary Gunderson, a graduate of Wake Forest University and a seminarian at Emory University, cochaired the committee.

Their first step was to mail a hunger newsletter called *Seeds* in 1977 to 800 Southern Baptists. Their second step was to push a resolution through the Southern Baptist Convention asking its agencies to consider hosting a hunger convocation. They succeeded at both.

Loving and Gunderson continued mailing newsletters until February 1979 when the first issue of *Seeds* as a magazine appeared. For the next two years, it appeared ten times annually. Beginning in 1981, *Seeds* changed its format. It became a bimonthly magazine with a bulletin-type publication called *Sprouts* appearing on alternate months.

Originally, *Seeds* identified itself as a magazine for Southern Baptists concerned about world hunger. In October 1982 it broadened its constituency to Christians concerned about hunger, yet retained a special focus on Southern Baptists. The December 1986 issue reflected a step in a new direction, away from being a ministry of Oakhurst Baptist Church to being a nonprofit corporation. Southern Baptists still represent a large percentage of those on the board of directors.

Who subscribes to *Seeds?*

The vast majority of subscribers are Christian laypeople. Thirty-four percent of the subscribers are equally divided between Catholics and Presbyterians, according to a 1987 readership survey. Sixteen percent of the readers identified themselves as Lutherans. Eleven percent were Methodist and 10 percent were Baptists.

What is the source of *Seeds'* income and how is it spent?

In 1987, *Seeds'* operating budget was over $398,000. Its single largest source of income was contributions from members, totaling slightly less than $200,000. Its typesetting business, a tent-making dimension of the organization, provided $114,000. Subscriptions and publications accounted for another $73,000. No funds came from government sources.

An estimated $160,000 went for salaries. Another $70,000 was spent on printing and promotional costs. Less than $10,000 was allocated for travel. An audited financial statement is available upon request.

What has *Seeds* accomplished?

Seeds has twice won the prestigious World Hunger Media Award (1982 and 1986). On both occasions, it has been singled out for the best coverage of world hunger by any periodical in the nation. Considering the many influential weekly magazines, including newsmagazines with tremendous budgets and huge staffs, *Seeds'* accomplishment is impressive.

Less glamorous, yet more important, is the fact that *Seeds* has become part of the main diet for those working against hunger at home and abroad. Its readers are the leaders and activists in the hunger movement.

For more information, write *Seeds*, 222 East Lake Drive, Decatur, GA 30030.

Conclusion

Bread for the World, Habitat for Humanity, and *Seeds* stand in the frontlines in the battle against hunger. Since they do not engage the emergency relief and development programs which many denominations have, they provide Christian laypersons concerned about hunger with additional avenues for involvement. Moreover, their work does not duplicate nor compete with that of local churches. Instead, it extends and strengthens those efforts.

[1]*Annual Report* 1986, International Fund for Agricultural Development, 7.

[2]Frances Moore Lappé and Joseph Collins, *World Hunger: Twelve Myths* (New York: Grove Press, Inc., 1986), 9.

[3]Henry Kissinger quoted by Arthur Simon in *Christian Faith and Public Policy: No Grounds for Divorce* (Grand Rapids: William B. Eerdmans Publishing Company, 1987), 44-45.

[4]Millard Fuller, *Bokotola* (Piscataway, N.J.: Association Press, 1977), 18.

[5]Millard Fuller and Diane Scott, *Love in the Mortar Joints* (Piscataway, N.J.: Association Press, 1980), 91-92.

[6]Kathleen Hayes, "Millard Fuller: Building Houses for Humanity," *Other Side*, January/February 1986, 12.

Recommended Reading List

Bobo, Kimberly. *Lives Matter: A Handbook for Christian Organizing.* Kansas City: Sheed and Ward, 1986.

Freudenberger, C. Dean. *Food for Tomorrow?* Minneapolis: Augsburg Publishing House, 1984.

Fuller, Millard, and Diane Scott. *No More Shacks*! Waco: Word Books, 1986.

Harrison, Paul. *The Greening of Africa: Breaking Through in the Battle for Land and Food.* New York: Penguin Books, 1987.

Lappé, Frances Moore, Joseph Collins, and David Kinley. *Aid as Obstacle: Twenty Questions About Our Foreign Aid and the Hungry.* San Francisco: Food First, 1980.

Lappé, Frances Moore, and Joseph Collins. *World Hunger: Twelve Myths.* New York: Grove Press, Inc., 1986.

Lutz, Charles P., ed. *Farming the Lord's Land: Christian Perspectives on American Agriculture.* Minneapolis: Augsburg Publishing House, 1980.

Nelson, Jack A. *Hunger for Justice: The Politics of Food and Faith.* Maryknoll, N. Y.: Orbis Books, 1982.

Sider, Ronald J. *Cry Justice: The Bible on Hunger and Poverty.* New York: Paulist Press, 1980.

____________. *Rich Christians in an Age of Hunger: A Bible Study.* 2d Rev. Ed. Downers Grove, Ill.: Inter-Varsity Press, 1984.

Simon, Arthur. *Bread for the World. Rev. Ed.* New York: Paulist Press, 1984.

____________. *Christian Faith and Public Policy: No Grounds for Divorce.* Grand Rapids: William B. Eerdmans Publishing Company, 1987.

Timberlake, Lloyd. *Africa in Crisis: The Causes, the Cures of Environmental Bankruptcy.* Washington, D.C.: International Institute for Environment and Development, 1985.

Toton, Suzanne C. *World Hunger: The Responsibility of Christian Education.* Maryknoll, N. Y.: Orbis Books, 1982.

Withers, Leslie, and Tom Peterson, eds. *Hunger Action Handbook: What You Can Do and How to Do It.* Decatur, Georgia: *Seeds* Magazine, 1987.

Recommended Southern Baptist Periodicals

Royal Service. Published by Woman's Missionary Union, P.O. Box C-10, Birmingham, AL 35283-0010.

Contempo. Published by Woman's Missionary Union, P.O. Box C-10, Birmingham, Alabama 35283-0010.

World Mission Journal. Published by Brotherhood Commission, 1548 Poplar Avenue, Memphis, TN 38140.

Light. Published by Christian Life Commission, 901 Commerce Street, Suite 550, Nashville, TN 37203.

The Commission. Published by the Foreign Mission Board, P.O. Box 6767, Richmond, VA 30367.

MissionsUSA. Published by the Home Mission Board, 1350 Spring Street, NW, Atlanta, GA 30367-5601.

BROADMAN
B P
SUPPLIES
Date Due